Reading together

RETHINKING READING

Series Editor: L. John Chapman
School of Education, The Open University

Reading together

ROBIN CAMPBELL

Open University Press
Milton Keynes · Philadelphia

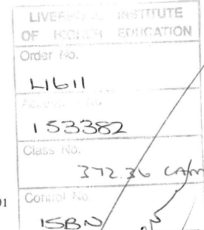

Open University Press
Celtic Court
22 Ballmoor
Buckingham MK18 1XW

and
1900 Frost Road, Suite 101
Bristol, PA 19007, USA

First Published 1990

Copyright © Robin Campbell 1990

British Library Cataloguing in Publication Data

Campbell, Robin, 1937-
    Reading together. — (Rethinking reading).
    1. Children, 5–11 years. Reading skills. Teaching
    I. Title   II. Series
    372.4

    ISBN 0-335-09450-3
    ISBN 0-335-09449-X pbk

Library of Congress Cataloging-in-Publication Data

Campbell, Robin, 1937-
    Reading together/Robin Campbell.
    p. cm. -- (Rethinking reading)
    Includes bibliographical references.
    ISBN 0-335-09450-3. -- ISBN 0-335-09449-X (pbk.)
    1. Reading (Elementary) 2. Reading (Elementary)--Case studies.
    I. Title.   II. Series.
    LB1573.C198 1990   90-35679
    372.4--dc20   CIP

Typeset by Burns & Smith Limited, Derby
Printed in Great Britain by St Edmundsbury Press
Bury St Edmunds, Suffolk

Contents

Acknowledgements

A central theme of this book is that children develop as readers in interaction with an adult/teacher who provides guidance and support for that developing reading. As the author of the book I recognize that the ideas that are expressed here are also the outcome of interactions with many colleagues, teachers and children about reading. I owe a debt of gratitude to all of those people who have supported me in my development. It is of course impossible to name all those who provided support, first, because there are so many from who I have learned and, second, because in naming some others are inevitably and unfortunately omitted.

Nevertheless as the reader reads this book the debt that is due to Ken and Yetta Goodman, Elizabeth Goodacre, Margaret Meek, etc.... and to Kirsty, Robert, Brian, Leah, etc.... will become evident. Fellow teachers, children, and of course my family, have made this book possible.

In addition the author and publisher would wish to thank the following for permission to reproduce copyright material in this book: The Bodley Head, *Bertie at the Dentist* by P. Bouma, *Goodnight Owl* by P. Hutchins and *Whistle for Willie* by E.J. Keats; Heinemann Educational Books, *I Can Jump* by J. Cowley; Schofield and Sims Ltd, *No Ducklings for Breakfast* – Jumping Off Book One; Frederick Warne, *Dizzy Dog*, Sunshine Books.

CHAPTER 1

Introduction

This book is about children learning to read. It is also about the process and interaction that occurs between the child and an adult/teacher in order to facilitate such learning. Indeed it is a central premise of this text that the crucial features of learning to read can be seen in the interaction between the adult and the child in a number of different literacy events. These literacy events involve a book (or books) and the child and adult reading together in some form or other. As Frank Smith has suggested in order 'to learn to read children need to read' (1978, p5). And as Smith then noted the issue is both as simple and as difficult as that. What such a view implies is the need for books/interesting materials that are meaningful to the learner and a facilitating, guiding adult working alongside and together with the learner. Or as Kenneth Goodman stated 'children should be read to and with' (1986, p44).

The task is therefore quite simple. All that is required is interesting reading material and an adult to work together with the child. However the difficulty is; What does this mean? What type of reading activities can and do take place? How does the adult work alongside and with the young learner? What sort of guidance is the adult to give to the child?

A range of activities which involve an adult reader, a child learner and a book are apparent. Initially this might involve the adult reading to the child, although as we shall note subsequently it is never only to the child. From the earliest stages of an adult reading to the young learner, the story reading can be seen as an interaction which suggests that the reading is with, rather than solely to, the child (Cochran-Smith, 1984). The child responds to the story, to the reader's intonations and to questions, as well as putting forward ideas of his/her own. These responses and initiations by the learner eventually lead to a stage where the reading is more of a shared reading in which the adult reads with the child and each contributes to the reading from the text (Waterland, 1985). Subsequently the child begins to develop an even more major role within the interaction and the adult becomes more of a listener to the child's reading. However, hearing children read does not lessen the demands made upon the adult (Campbell, 1988a). The role of listening to the reading, responding to the miscues and structuring the interaction all require careful thought. Listening is not a passive activity, it is something which requires the adult's full attention. Eventually the young learners will want to spend much of their time reading silently for themselves. At home the children will create their own time and space for such readings. At school it may be that periods of time will be set aside for Sustained Silent Reading (SSR) in some format.

The sequence of reading together which is suggested therefore is:

Story reading – adult reads to children,
Shared reading – adult and child read together,
Hearing children read – child reads to adult,
Sustained silent reading – child reads to self.

This sequence is also suggested, in part, by Chapman (1987) who refers to reading to and with the children as a methodology to enable children to develop as readers.

Of course the suggested sequence should not be seen as a rigid set of stages to be followed by each child with each stage completed before moving on to the next stage. Children will be involved with each of the elements throughout childhood. The youngest of children will be seen 'reading' a picture book even though the print is not yet understood fully, and this might be regarded as being involved in a period of sustained silent reading. Similarly a class of older junior children will still welcome story reading sessions where an interesting book is read well by their teacher. However what may be apparent is the gradual trend from the youngest child listening to an adult read as his/her predominant literacy event to the older child whose main literacy activity becomes the silent reading to oneself.

The notion of reading together which is presented in this book can be seen to be linked to a perspective on literacy development which has become increasingly influential in the last decade or so. This perspective emphasizes whole language, emergent literacy and interactions. Goodman (1986) is one of the key figures in this movement and his psycholinguistic research leads him to argue for a whole language approach to literacy. Meaningful texts which allow the reader to predict possibilities and to construct meaning during reading would be suggested as being important. Therefore, the adult and child reading together from an interesting book rather than being concerned with the isolation and teaching of skills would be part of the learning experience. Smith (1978) and Meek (1982) are two influential writers who also have argued for the importance of meaningful books as a key factor in encouraging literacy development. Furthermore Meek argued that for the learning to be successful the adult/child interaction had to be one of genuine sharing. This genuine sharing or reading together in its various forms provides the basis from which the child's literacy can emerge. The child makes sense of the information that is seen and heard, and gradually over a period of time literacy is developed or emerges (Hall, 1987). To some teachers and parents this might suggest that the teacher is no longer teaching. However, it really is dependent upon how the word teaching is defined. If teaching is perceived as a process of direct instruction having first determined the skills to be taught then reading together does not involve teaching. However, if teaching is perceived within an interactional perspective (Wells, 1985) in which the crucial role of the adult/teacher is to sustain, encourage and facilitate the child in his/her self-activated learning then reading together is very much concerned with the process of teaching and learning. Indeed the role of the adult is of considerable importance and is a complex one which demands genuine collaboration, careful support and subtle mediation often of a non-directive nature. Shared meanings and understandings are negotiated during this teaching and learning process.

Thus reading together is a simple concept but one in which the role of the adult/teacher and the young learner is complex and changing according to the nature of the activity which is taking place. In order to make sense of those activities which are suggested in this book and to explore in greater depth the contribution of both adult and child within the reading together interactions a number of classroom extracts have been used as exemplars. That is not to suggest that the examples which are given provide a model of appropriate behaviour. However the examples, all of which are taken from normal classrooms in primary schools, do allow for a discussion of the activities within a practical framework rather than being offered solely as a theoretical statement. And they do indicate possible approaches that the adult/teacher might utilize, together with a child, in order to encourage the reading development of the young learner.

CHAPTER 2

Story reading

Although story reading is put forward as the first part of the reading together sequence this is not to suggest that reading only starts at that point in the classroom or home. A child will also have been learning to read the environmental print of society. So the child will have 'read' from the corn-flakes packet, shop signs, T.V. programmes, etc., guided by a parent. Therefore some knowledge of print, words, sentences and meaning will already have been assimilated by most children. This knowledge will help each child to make sense of stories during story readings and also form the foundations from which reading, with ever increasing independence, can develop. However, it is story reading as part of a reading together sequence that will now be explored.

There is a substantial and growing literature which notes the importance of story reading in the early years of education. That literature led Teale (1984) to conclude that there was now overwhelming evidence to suggest that story reading has facilitative effects on literacy development. Part of that evidence was derived from the longitudinal Children Learning to Read project in Bristol. Arising out of that project Wells (1986) noted that listening to stories, and taking part in discussions about them, was significantly associated with a subsequent development of literacy. However, Wells argued that listening to a story read to a whole class was not necessarily an answer. For some children who might not be ready to attend to written language in impersonal conditions a one-to-one interaction with an adult centered on a story, as might have been experienced by many children at home, was required. White (1984) had also argued for the one-to-one interactions of story reading as a foundation for subsequent literacy development. Furthermore she suggested that the task of reading to more than one, as in an infant classroom, would be difficult. Two questions might therefore need to be answered. Is it possible to read stories to a class of children with a variety of backgrounds and story reading experiences? and, Would a class story reading provide a worthwhile experience for all the children? Dombey (1988) provides a positive response to such questions. She utilized an example, drawn from a nursery classroom of three- and four-year olds in which many of the children had not had a significant amount of sharing stories from books at home, to demonstrate how reading to a class can be successful and worthwhile. However, in order to succeed there was a need for a high level of planning by the teacher. This was specially the case for two reasons. First, the children were being asked to make sense of language which was independent of its physical context and second, the children all had different interests, experiences and ideas about the world. Nevertheless the teacher provided a literacy event that was worthwhile. But in what sense is story reading seen as worthwhile? What might children gain from such a literacy activity?

Story reading provides a gateway into the world of literacy. It offers a range of features which will encourage literacy development within the child. First, and perhaps most importantly, it introduces children to the enjoyment of reading (Meek, 1984). Providing that the teacher has given consideration to the environment for the story reading then a positive, secure and enjoyable atmosphere will prevail (Trelease, 1984). The children will then associate reading with pleasure (Strickland and Morrow, 1989) and will be encouraged to listen attentively to the stories and to want to read for themselves. The enjoyment of the story reading will promote an interest in books (Hudson, 1988); it is therefore important that the teacher pays careful attention to the selection of books that are read to the class. That selection can offer insights into the literacy and cultural heritage of society and can serve to socialize into certain attitudes and values. It can also provide a wide range of experience. These experiences may provide a source of play activities for the child (White, 1984). They will stimulate the imagination as well as creating the opportunity for emotional, social and psychological growth (Trelease, 1984). However, such a view again serves to remind us of how important the selection of the books that will be read to the class is. Jim Trelease argued that not only will the teacher have read the book in order to prepare for the story reading but will also have considered, for instance, the emotional impact of the story and will try to avoid reading from books which might be above the emotional level of the child. In terms of motivation towards reading, creating enjoyment, developing an interest in books and encouraging emotional, social and psychological development story reading has an enormous amount to offer. And yet story reading does even more because it also teaches about language.

Part of the knowledge about language that is acquired is that the child learns how books work (Meek, 1984). Therefore the child will know how to handle a book, will know about front-to-back and left-to-right directionality (Strickland and Morrow, 1989). This knowledge will be acquired not because it has been taught directly but because the child will be involved in a constructive process of making sense of stories and books during the shared experiences of story reading with a supportive teacher (Cochran-Smith, 1984). As well as knowing about books the child will become aware of story structure (Teale, 1984). Although the child is unlikely to be able to talk about the consistent use of past tense, story opening, story ending, characters, setting and plot, nevertheless such knowledge is being acquired and will increasingly be evident in the child's own attempts to tell or write a story.

There are other aspects of language which will be stimulated by story reading. Quite simply the child will learn new words. So a growth of vocabulary will become apparent. However, as Dombey (1988) has argued it is not only new words but also new syntactic forms, new meanings and new ways of organizing discourse that are taken on simultaneously. The child will be learning about the organization of written language and as Wells (1986) suggested its characteristic rhythms and structures. This, he argued, would mean that the child would find the language familiar when an attempt was made to read a book for oneself.

If so much is going to be learnt from and during story reading then it would appear that, as Chapman (1987) noted, story reading in the classroom may be a skilled job. The teacher may wish to show book and print features during the story reading, according to the age of the children, but, very importantly, without detracting from the enjoyment of the story. A fine and skilled balance in the reading is necessary. However it may be that certain incidental learning will also occur. The children will learn about intonation patterns and emphases. The well-prepared teacher will provide a model of meaningful reading for the listeners. This meaningful reading will, of course, be determined in part by the careful selection of books which will stimulate and sustain the children's attention and interest (Wade, 1982). In part this selection will allow the teacher to create a wholeness to each reading session (Meek, 1984), a beginning and ending will be apparent. Of course with older children the ending of any one read may be at a natural point in the story which also provides the starting point for the next day's reading. For younger children the story will be completed during one session.

As has been implied, story reading is too important to be an infrequent feature of classroom life. Story reading has so much to offer that it must surely be a daily event. And not as a ritualized ending of the school day, although that time could be used for story reading. Whatever time is used for story reading the event has to be presented with enthusiasm and interest by the teacher. Trelease (1984) provided a comprehensive list of do's and don'ts of reading aloud. He actually suggested the setting aside of at least one traditional time each day for a story which might be before leaving school. However alongside this were other important features such as preparing for the story reading, previewing the book by reading it to oneself, not reading to the class if you did not enjoy it yourself, reading with expression, thinking about pacing – read slowly enough and other features. What all the do's and don'ts added up to was the need for the teacher to think about preparation, organization, thoughtful reading, enthusiasm and a shared enjoyment of the story.

No matter how well prepared the teacher might be there will be interruptions to the reading, especially from the younger children. Trelease suggests that the teacher must avoid being unnerved by such interruptions. Meek (1984) extends this view by suggesting that parents become very skilled at keeping the flow going. Teachers too even with a large class can become skillful at using the interruptions, developing them perhaps and then moving the story on. Always in mind is the view that the nature of the interaction will be a crucial feature in the learning which takes place (Wells, 1985). A genuine collaborative interaction in which guidance and a responsiveness to the children's needs are evident will be part of the teacher's role. Eventually, and particularly as the children become older, interruptions become less frequent and story reading becomes more of a reading and listening event. Such a development is very gradual, however what can be discerned is the continuum from story readings with frequent interruptions by young children and a careful and responsive use of these interruptions by the teacher to a stage where the story reading is very largely not interrupted and a discussion about the story may occur after the reading.

So what would such interactions look like in the classroom? In order to make sense of story reading interactions two classroom examples will be considered in some detail. The first of these examples is taken from a reception classroom of five-year-old children where the children are very involved in the story and frequently interrupt the teacher. The second example also from that infant classroom, but of the children now older, six years, at the end of the school year, is more demonstrative of children whose involvement is no less but who listen attentively to the story and then take part in a discussion about the story at the end of the session.

An early story reading session

In this reception classroom the five-year-old children were already in the library corner sitting on the carpet, something which will have required

careful teacher organization, their teacher was sitting on a chair in front of them and was ready to start the story reading.

Teacher: Shall we have the story of 'Bertie at the Dentist's'?
Children: [Laughter]
Teacher: Who do you think Bertie is?
          Sonny?
Sonny: Hippopotamus.
Teacher: He's a hippopotamus.
          Do you think he's a real one?
Children: No.
          A toy one.
Teacher: Richard, what do you think?
Richard: A toy one.
Teacher: A toy one.
          Shall we see what happens to 'Bertie at the Dentist's'?
             Bertie was Thomas's toy hippo. They went
             everywhere together. On the day that
             Thomas had to go to the dentist's
             for a check up, he took Bertie along.
          There he is taking Bertie.
Michael: Bertie can't walk.
Teacher: No Bertie can't walk can he?
             'Hop up here, Thomas,' said the
             dentist.
             'Let's take a look.'
             Thomas climbed on to the dentist's
             chair.
Richard: It goes up.
Teacher: It does go up doesn't it Richard, yes.
             Bertie sat on his tummy and
             watched. The chair sank back. Then it
             shot up into the air.
Children: [Laughter]
Teacher: Bertie nearly fell off.
Katrina: He didn't though.
Teacher: No, he didn't.
          Why do you think he nearly fell off?
Katrina: Because he's on the edge of the arm.
Teacher: He nearly fell over the edge of the arm, yes.

In the initial part of this story reading interaction two main segments were apparent. First there was the preparation for listening in which the teacher talked with the children about the book to be read. In this example the teacher simply provided the title of the story and introduced the main character, Bertie the hippo. However, the introduction of Bertie was done by involving the children with the use of some questions. Now although it could be argued that a longer prereading discussion might have taken place nevertheless it has to be recognized that with very young children it is the story line which will be important, it is not inappropriate therefore to have a quick start to the story. Furthermore the teacher will have been making judgements about the attention of the children and other non-verbal aspects and would have used that information in determining when to start reading. Once started on the reading, the second segment, the teacher took the opportunity to introduce another character and re-introduce Bertie with her comment 'There he is taking Bertie'. She also responded to the comments of Michael, Richard and Katrina therefore demonstrating her responsiveness to the children's thinking. The amount of detail that the children take from the text and the illustrations can be noted from Katrina's response that Bertie nearly fell off 'Because he's on the edge of the arm'. The teacher confirmed that interpretation and then continued to read.

Teacher: 'You sit here, Bertie,' said the dentist.
                 He began to wash his hands.
                 Why do you think he washes his hands?
                 Why does he?
Helen: So you don't get germs.
Teacher: So you don't get germs, that's right. He has to be all lovely and clean. And as Clare said he washes with the soap.
                 Bertie was fascinated. He had never
                 seen soap in a bottle before.
Robert: I have.
Teacher: You have.
Children: I have.
Robert: I've seen hair washes.
Teacher: You've seen what?
Robert: Hair washes.
Teacher: What do we call hair washes? Don't call out.
                 Hair- what do we call it? In a bottle, Hair?
Sarah: Hair shampoo.
Teacher: Hair shampoo.
John: I've seen it coming out of taps.
Teacher: You've seen soap coming out of taps, yes that's right.
                 What do you have to do John?
John: Wash your hands.

Teacher:	Yes, but what do you do to the tap? Do you know?
John:	You press the thing in.
Teacher:	You usually have to press it that's right.
John:	And it comes down on to your hands.
Teacher:	That's right, yes. Shall we see what happens next at the dentist's. When the dentist was not looking, Bertie wrote a big
Children:	Buh, B.
Teacher:	Buh or a B, yes. 'B' on the mirror with the soap. Thomas frowned at him.
Children:	Oh!
Louise:	He's got soap all over his hands.
Teacher:	He has hasn't he. The dentist began examining Thomas's teeth with a little mirror.
Keith:	He took it out.
Teacher:	Bertie spotted an enormous pair of dentures. What are dentures? Gavin?
Gavin:	False teeth.
Teacher:	They are false teeth. Who might need false teeth?
Gavin:	The hippopotamus.
Teacher:	The hippopotamus might but who else might, Michael?
Michael:	Thomas.
Teacher:	Thomas might but do you think he will?
Children:	No.
Teacher:	Who might need false teeth? Fay?
Fay:	The boy.
Teacher:	The boy might, anybody else. Who else might need false teeth?
Fay:	The mum.
Teacher:	The mum might or the?
Children:	The dad.
Gavin:	Another customer.
Teacher:	The dad or another customer Gavin, yes. Bertie spotted an enormous pair of dentures. They looked as if they might fit . . .
John:	He put them in.

Teacher: . . . THEY DID!
                      Thomas glared at him.
Children: Oh!
Teacher: 'You should always brush your teeth
                      thoroughly,' the dentist told Thomas.
                      Bertie came upon a large toothbrush
                      and some toothpaste.
Mark: Toothpaste, he's going to brush his teeth.
Teacher: He is indeed Mark.
                      In no time he had
                      brushed up a glorious foam.
Teacher/Children [Together they go through the action of brushing
           teeth.]
Children: [Laughter].

As the teacher read from the book a substantial number of child comments and demonstrations of involvement became apparent and the teacher also asked questions about the reading. Indeed the transcription shows the reading embedded in a very substantial dialogue between the teacher and the children. The teacher was attempting to maintain a flow in the reading but at the same time remaining responsive to the needs and interests of the class. At times the teacher asked questions about aspects of the story. In part they were questions of fact 'What do we call hair washes?' but they also included questions which required the children to predict 'Who might need false teeth?'. However at other points it was the comments from the children; Robert 'I have [seen soap in a bottle]' and John 'I've seen it coming out of taps' that were used by the teacher to extend language and meaning.

Two other interruptions were of particular interest. First, there was the occasion where the children demonstrated their developing knowledge of letter sounds and names 'Buh, B' which the teacher confirmed but did not develop as that might have been to detract from the story line and meaning. Second, there was the non-verbal involvement with the story as the children and the teacher together went through the action of brushing teeth. The text was related to personal life experiences albeit non-verbally. The teacher was able to encourage a contextualization of the story and therefore to enhance meaning. The involvement with the actions of the story also created laughter and enjoyment of the story line.

The teacher continued to read the story and despite the many interruptions she maintained a flow to the reading. However as well as attempting to keep the reading moving she also paused briefly at natural breaks, the end of a sentence and the end of a page, which allowed the children to comment, question and to react. She also reinforced the responses from the children and occasionally asked questions of fact or prediction (Strickland and Morrow, 1989). The dialogue continued in a manner similar to that which has been debated above.

Teacher:	Thomas
	squirmed in his chair.
	Why do you think Thomas squirmed in the chair?
Clare:	He was laughing.
Teacher:	He was laughing.
Clare:	'Cos it was funny to see.
Teacher:	It might have been funny to see.
Clare:	'Cos he had never seen a hippo brush his teeth.
Teacher:	Probably because he had never seen a hippopotamus brush his teeth.
	That's right.
	The dentist pulled some dental
	floss to clean between Thomas's teeth.
	Does anybody know what dental floss is?
	What is dental floss?
	Those of you who have been to the dentist might know.
	What is it Gavin?
Gavin:	A string you put in between your teeth.
Teacher:	That's right like string you put in between your teeth to clean right between your teeth.
Gavin:	Like my mum's got at home.
Teacher:	Your mummy's got it at home too.
	Right.
	Bertie watched, entranced. He liked
	the way it came out of the container,
	brr..
	It just whips out doesn't it?
	but
	it was some time before he discovered
	how to cut it off.
	What had Bertie done with the dental floss?
Gavin:	Covered it all over him.
Teacher:	Yes, Gavin he had tied it all over him.
	And when was he able to stop?
Gavin:	When ...
Teacher:	When it what?
Gavin:	When it was all finished do you think or when something else?
Jay:	When the batteries had finished.
Teacher:	When the batteries had finished. I thought it was something

	else that told us when.
Gavin:	Batteries.
Teacher:	They don't have batteries, not really. But when did it stop?
Helen:	When he got tangled up.
Teacher:	He had got tangled up. But when was he able to stop being tangled up? When he what?
Helen:	When it was all done.
Teacher:	No.
Michael:	When the little boy was doing something.
Teacher:	No, not when the little boy was doing something. When he had?
Michael:	When he learned something.
Teacher:	When he learnt what?
Keith:	That he shouldn't do it.
Teacher:	When he learnt that he mustn't do it. Not quite. When he learned …
Keith:	To brush his teeth.
Teacher:	No.
Michael:	When he learned a lesson.
Teacher:	Not when he learned a . . . I'll read it to you shall I?

> it was some time before he discovered
> how to cut it off.

	He'd learnt?
Jennifer:	With scissors.
Teacher:	No, what does it have? Does anyone know what the dental floss has to cut it off?
Sarah:	A needle.
Teacher:	Not a needle.
Gavin:	A metal thing.
Teacher:	That's right. It's on the container a little metal thing that you can cut it with.

> Thomas made frantic signs at him
> from behind the dentist's back.

	Oh dear.
Louise:	He was trying to stop him.
Teacher:	He was trying to make him stop it.

> 'You should not eat too many
> sweets,' said the dentist. Bertie found
> some sugar-free gum in the cupboard.

	Phew.
Children:	[Laughter]
Teacher:	And

> He blew a large bubble.

Phew.
Thomas closed his eyes, braced
himself and waited ...

Richard: It burst.
Teacher: Do you think it popped?
Children: Yes, popped.
Teacher: POP!
Children: POP. POP. POP. POP. POP. POP.
Teacher: 'What was that?' said the dentist.
Luckily he had the wrong specs on and
couldn't see Bertie cleaning the gum off
his nose.
'No cavities, young man. You can get
down. Don't forget Bertie,' said the
dentist.
Thomas left in a hurry.
Why do you think he left Mark, in a hurry?
Mark: Because he didn't want to get told off.
Teacher: He didn't want to get told off.
Who might have told him off?
Mark: The dentist . . . his mum.
Teacher: Why?
Mark: He'd been playing about with things he shouldn't have been.
Teacher: Yes, he'd been playing around with things he shouldn't have
been.
His little sister, Tessa, was waiting for
him.
'Were you scared?' she asked.
'No I wasn't,' said Thomas. 'And nor
was Bertie!'
There.

A central feature of this section of the story reading, which led up to
the completion of the story, was the extended dialogue which occurred
around the topic of dental floss. The teacher had asked a series of questions
concerned with three aspects of dental floss in the story. First, 'What is
dental floss?' a question which required the children to use their prior
knowledge and experiences outside the context of the story. That question
was soon answered. The second question, 'What had Bertie done with the
dental floss?' required an involvement and understanding of the story, and
again the question was soon answered. The third question, 'And when was
he able to stop?' required the children to use their prior knowledge about
dental floss containers, to use their understanding of the story and

especially the sentence 'He liked the way it came out of the container, but it was some time before he discovered how to cut it off.' and to be able to relate this sentence to the question which was framed somewhat differently. Perhaps because of this the children took some time and prompting before the answer was given. Once the answer had been received the teacher attempted to recreate a balance between reading from the book and responding to the children's questions or comments. The last 21 lines of the text were read without a substantial dialogue taking place about the story. Of course the teacher did still ask questions, 'Do you think it popped?', responded to comments, 'He was trying to make him stop it.', provided actions outside of the story, 'Phew' to blow a bubble which involved the children in the story and encouraged the children to become storytellers with her 'POP'. As Chapman (1987) suggested story reading in the classroom demands skill. The teacher needs to get a balance between reading and a dialogue with the listeners, in part that is achieved by the careful preparation for the story reading (Trelease, 1984). Or to take an interactional perspective (Wells, 1985) the teacher will constantly be seeking to encourage and facilitate the learners involvement with the story.

Another two features were also apparent in the story reading before the teacher reached the topic of dental floss. Although at the beginning of the story the teacher had questioned the children about the hippopotamus and established that it was a toy one this did not stop the teacher and the children, once they were fully involved with the story, from agreeing that Thomas had probably not seen 'a hippo brush his teeth'. Reality could be suspended during the involvement with the story. Second, Dombey (1988) noted that children would learn about new ways of organizing discourse during story readings. They would also learn about aspects of discourse via the interaction with the teacher. At one point the teacher had concluded an exchange then indicated a boundary in the discourse by the use of a marker 'right' (Sinclair and Coulthard, 1975) before continuing with the reading of the story. Over a period of time that and other aspects of discourse would be learnt by the children.

The teacher had indicated the end of the story with her emphatic 'There.' The interaction was then concluded:

Teacher: Did you like that story?
Children: Yes, yes, yes.
Sarah: It was lovely.
Teacher: It was lovely.
Children: Yes.
Helen: Yes, it was very nice.
Teacher: Now what did you like about it Clare.
Clare: I liked the bit when the bubble popped.

Teacher: When the bubble popped.
Robert: I liked the bit where . . . he got covered up in the floss.
Teacher: Right, now listen.
Why do you think Thomas took Bertie to the dentist?
Why do you think Audrey?
Audrey: Because he loved Bertie.
Teacher: Because he loved Bertie.
Anybody else, any other reason?
Jennifer: Because he was eating too many sweets.
Teacher: Who was?
Jennifer: Bertie.
Teacher: Bertie was? And that's why he took him to the dentist?
He might have done, yes.
Fay.
Fay: Because he ate too many sweets.
Teacher: So that's why he took him to the dentist.
Right.
Why do you think Bertie did all these things?
Why do you think Bertie did them?
Why do you think Sabrina?
Sabrina: Because he never had none teeth.
Teacher: Why did Bertie do all those things?
Richard: He was copying the doctor.
Teacher: He was copying the ...
Children: Doctor, doctor, dentist.
Teacher: Dentist that's right. He was copying the dentist.
And what else? Why else was he doing all these different things?
Fay.
Fay: He was trying to make fun.
Teacher: Yes, he was trying to make fun any other reason?
Audrey.
Audrey: Because he liked it.
Teacher: Because he liked it, right.
Why didn't the dentist notice what Bertie was doing?
Michael: He was too busy looking at Thomas.
Teacher: He was too busy looking at Thomas, but was there another reason why he didn't notice?
John.
John: Because he had the wrong glasses on.
Teacher: Good boy, because he had the wrong glasses on that's right.
And finally, why did Thomas want to leave in such a hurry with Bertie.

Keith: Because he didn't want to get told off.
Teacher: He didn't want to get told off by whom?
Children: The dentist.
Teacher: The dentist.
Why would the dentist have told Thomas off do you think?
Keith: Because he was playing with the things.
Teacher: Who was?
Children: Thomas . . . the dentist . . .
Teacher: No Thomas wasn't playing.
Children: Bertie.
Teacher: Bertie was playing that's right.
He wanted to get out very quickly.
Keith: Or he might have got told off.
Teacher: Or he might have got told off.
That's lovely.
Well done children.

The concluding exchanges began with questions about the enjoyment of the story. After all, the activity may have as a prime purpose the encouragement of the enjoyment of reading (Meek, 1984). The teacher also related the story to the children's own experiences and asked questions about the story. In part, the questions were of the 'What?' and 'Who?' type but they also more frequently were asking 'Why?' and therefore required the children to reason rather than simply to recall. And finally the interaction was brought to an end by the teacher praising the children and indicating the finish partly by words and partly by the use of appropriate intonational patterns.

This class of five-year-old children were very involved with the story and their involvement led them to interrupt or actively participate in the story reading. Indeed both the children and the teacher interrupted the story from time to time in order to comment or to question. And the teacher used the children's questions and comments to develop the interaction. However, as the children become older they are encouraged to adopt a role more akin to that of an audience and to listen to the story, a feature which Heath (1982) also found to be evident at home. An example of the teacher reading to the children now aged six will be provided.

A later story reading session

In this example the teacher had again organized the children so that they were in the library corner of the room and seated comfortably ready to listen to the story. Perhaps because the children were now accustomed to listening to stories as a group on a regular and frequent basis, the teacher did not have a discussion of the book before she started to read. The story could provide for the children the meaning, coherence and fulfilment. Indeed the story that the teacher was to read to the class was one which had been used by Wade (1982) to note the sustenance that could be provided by a well written story.

Teacher: Whistle for Willie.
Children: [Laughter]
Whistle for Willie.
Teacher: This is the story.
Oh, how Peter wished he could whistle!
Richard: He can't.
Children: Whew.
Teacher: He saw a boy playing with his dog. Whenever
the boy whistled, the dog ran straight to him.
Peter tried and tried to whistle, but he couldn't.
So instead he began to turn himself around,
around and around he whirled . . .
faster and faster . . .
When he stopped
everything turned
down . . .
and up . . .
and up . . .
and down . . .
and around
and around.
Children: [Laughter]
He's going dizzy.
Teacher: Peter saw his dog, Willie, coming.
Helen: He's walking away.
Teacher: Quick as a wink, he hid in an empty carton
lying on the pavement.
'Wouldn't it be funny if I whistled?' Peter thought.
'Willie would stop and look all around to see
who it was.'
Peter tried again to whistle
Children: Whew.
Keith: He's only blowing.
Teacher: but still he couldn't.
So Willie just walked on.

	Peter got out of the carton
	and started home.
	On the way he took some
	coloured chalks out of his pocket
	and drew a long, long line
Children:	[Laughter]
Louise:	He's being naughty.
Teacher:	right up to his door.
Children:	Oh!
Teacher:	He stood there and tried to whistle again.
	He blew till his cheeks were tired.
	But nothing happened.
Jay:	He still couldn't do it.
Teacher:	He went into his house and put on his father's
	old hat
Children:	[Laughter]
Teacher:	to make himself feel more grown-up.

A clear feature of this first half of the story reading was the way that the teacher maintained the story line and did not respond to the many comments from the children. The children were very involved with the story and laughed frequently at the antics of Peter. His whirling around which made him dizzy, chalking a line along the pavement and trying on his father's old hat all created amusement. The children also commented upon Peter's attempts to whistle and being naughty when he chalked on the pavement. Yet none of this received a teacher response. The teacher appeared to be encouraging the children to listen to the story and act like an audience. However what was also evident was the way in which the teacher accommodated the comments and responses of the children. Her reading fitted in with the children's involvement with the text. There was no need to reprimand the children for their interruptions, instead those comments and responses were listened to and then the teacher carried on with her reading. The excitement of the story was shared.

Teacher:	He looked into the mirror to practice whistling.
	Still no whistle!
	When his mother saw what he was doing,
	Peter pretended that he was his father.
	He said, 'I've come home early today, dear. Is Peter
	here?'
	His mother answered,
	'Why no, he's outside with Willie.'
	'Well, I'll go out and look for them,' said Peter.

John: Oh, he's dressed up as his daddy.
Teacher: First he walked along a crack in the pavement.
Children: [Laughter]
Teacher: Then he tried to run away from his shadow.
Michael: You can't.
Teacher: He jumped off his shadow.
      But when he landed
                  they were
                        together
                              again.

      He came to the corner
      where the carton was,
      and who should he see but Willie!
Children: Willie.
Teacher: Peter scrambled under the carton.
      He blew and blew and blew.
      Suddenly out came a real whistle!
Children: Whew.
Teacher: Willie stopped and looked around to see
      who it was.
Children: Oh.
Teacher: 'It's me,' Peter shouted, and stood up.
      Willie raced straight to him.
      Peter ran home
      to show his father and mother what he could do.
      They loved Peter's whistling.
Children: Whew.
Teacher: So did Willie.
      Peter's mother asked him and Willie
      to go an errand to the grocer's shop.
      He whistled all the way there,
      and he whistled all the way home.
Children: Whew.

So right up to the end of the story reading the children demonstrated their involvement with the story by whistling, or attempting to whistle, by commenting upon Peter's actions and indicating that you can't run away from your shadow. And all through the story reading the teacher maintained the story line and encouraged the children to behave as listeners. Furthermore this was the same teacher who in the earlier example had responded readily to the children's comments and questions and indeed had interrupted her own reading of the story to ask questions of the children. So the nature of the interaction had been changed during the course of the school year in a manner similar to that which Heath (1982) had noted in the home as children became older. However, although the story was offered without interruptions by the teacher, once that reading was completed the teacher then asked a series of questions about the text and engaged in a discussion with the children.

Teacher: What did Peter wish he could do?
Children: Whistle.
Teacher: Yes Sonny he wished he could whistle.
Why do you think he wished he could whistle? Why do you think Gavin?
Gavin: 'Cos he wanted his dog to come.
Teacher: He wanted his dog to come with him, yes. Clare?
Clare: He wanted his dog to come to him.
Teacher: Yes, that's right he wanted his dog to come to him.
Why did he want this?
Sarah: Because the boy.
Teacher: Yes, he wanted to copy the boy didn't he, that's right he'd seen a boy.
Why do you think Peter couldn't do it at first? Why do you think, Keith.
Keith: He didn't have his lips properly in place.
Teacher: He didn't have his lips properly in place. No he didn't.
Why don't you think he had his lips properly in place? Why do you think, Clare?
Clare: He wasn't blowing hard enough.
Teacher: No, he wasn't blowing hard enough, any other reason? Clare?
Clare: His lips were wet.
Teacher: Why do you think he couldn't do it at first, Sonny?
Sonny: When his lips were wet . . . umh . . .
Teacher: What wasn't he doing?
Sonny: Practising.
Teacher: Yes, he wasn't practising.
Sonny: He wasn't practising enough.
Teacher: No, but then what did happen when he did practise? Mark?
Mark: He managed.
Teacher: He did do it, yes, he did.

Although the teacher's first question was a 'What?' question which asked about the central theme of the story, 'What did Peter wish he could do?' she used this question as a means of moving into a series of questions which made greater demands. The first question was answered readily by a number of the children and was followed by a number of 'Why?' questions which required the children to reason, e.g. 'Why do you think

Peter couldn't do it at first?'. In some respects that question might be seen to be relating the story to the six-year-olds own experiences; how do you learn to whistle? And perhaps the final response from Sonny can be seen to be reflecting the ethos of a school, 'He wasn't practising enough.' In order to achieve you need to practise. However, as well as asking those 'Why?' questions the teacher also praised the children for their responses. That praise was given quite simply within the dialogue by the use of 'Yes', 'That's right' or by the teacher repeating the child's response and indicating the acceptability of the answer by that means. The interaction was completed in a similar manner with some further questioning.

Teacher: Now when Peter went home, what do you think Peter thought might happen when he put on his dad's hat?
What do you think Peter was going to think when he put on his dad's hat, Gavin?

Gavin: He could whistle.

Teacher: That he could whistle. Why?

Gavin: Because it made him look old.

Teacher: Because it made him look old, yes it did.
But did it work?

Children: No.

Teacher: No it didn't.
Where was Peter when he first learnt to whistle? Clare?

Clare: Outside.

Teacher: Outside where?

Clare: In the street.

Teacher: Outside in the street. Where was he?

Robert: In the park.

Teacher: I don't think he was in the park. Where was he in the street? Can you think where he was Sonny, can you remember?

Sonny: Next to his house.

Teacher: Mmh. Katrina?

Katrina: Next to the writing.

Teacher: Yes, but was he just in the street or was he doing something else?

Katrina: He was in the . . .

Teacher: Yes, he was under the what? What was it he was under?

Katrina: The box.

Teacher: Under the box, right.
Why was he under the box?

David: Because he wouldn't, he wouldn't see him then.

Teacher: Who wouldn't see him?

David: Willie the dog.

Teacher:	Willie the dog wouldn't see him and he learnt to whistle.
	Right.
	When Peter went to the grocers shop how do you think he felt?
	Sara?
Sara:	Happy, happy.
Teacher:	Why?
Sara:	'Cos he could whistle.
Teacher:	Yes, because he could whistle.
	Yes, he was very happy.

And so not only had the story finished on that happy note but the interaction shadowed the story by also finishing with a happy Peter. During the latter part of the interaction the teacher had again concentrated on questions that required more than just recall, although recall questions were evident. The teacher had also asked the children to reflect upon how Peter must have felt once he had been successful. Of course in this instance the teacher had used the time after the reading of the story to ask a series of questions albeit that those questions were most usually requiring the children to reason. Less opportunity was taken to get the children to retell some of the story, for the children to explore their thoughts about the events of the story and to comment upon them or for the children to express their enjoyment of the text and to initiate those comments. In addition only minimal use was made of text-to-life and life-to-text moves which helps the children to relate the story to their own experiences.

Of course this story reading is not presented as a model of what should be attempted, there were aspects that might have been developed, there were also elements which were quite positive. Indeed, seen in conjunction with the earlier interaction it is possible to detect how the teacher was attempting to guide the children as story listeners and gradually to become more of an audience while remaining involved with the story. What is evident is the way in which the story reading interaction had been developed over a number of interactions. And that certain key features need to be considered, these features are summarized below.

Summary

Story reading should not provide a ritualized finish to the school day; its contribution to a child's literacy development is so substantial (Teale, 1984) that it requires the teacher to prepare very carefully for the reading (Trelease, 1984). Part of this preparation involves the thoughtful selection of the books to be read (Wade, 1982).

The structure of the story readings will include first, an introduction

during which questions about the characters, plot or setting might prepare the children for the reading, second the story reading itself and finally a period of interaction during which questions are asked and feeling and comments from the children are evident (Flood, 1977). During early readings the teacher and the children will together create meaning and the active participation of the children will be noted (Dombey, 1988). Later the children will begin to adopt the role more of an audience (Heath, 1982).

Throughout the story readings the teacher will demonstrate that a real collaborative interaction is being provided. The teacher will be responsive to the needs of the listeners and will guide and facilitate their understanding of the text being read (Wells, 1985). And part of this responsiveness will be to demonstrate the enjoyment of reading (Meek, 1984) and the pleasure that can be found in books (Strickland and Morrow, 1989).

Dombey (1988) has argued that it is possible to provide a successful and worthwhile story reading with a whole class and not just a single child. The transcriptions provided above (and even more so the recordings with the sounds of children's enjoyment and participation) also suggest this to be the case.

What is evident during story reading is the children's involvement with the story and their apparent wish to share and be part of that story reading. Shared reading provides the setting where a child is invited to extend this involvement and to read some of the text. The next chapter considers shared reading in some detail.

CHAPTER 3

Shared reading

Although story reading might be seen as a time when the adult/teacher is reading to the children, the previous chapter demonstrated that the activity is really more of a reading together. The children are involved and contribute to the reading at various points. That involvement is extended during shared reading where the teacher encourages and guides the child towards reading some of the text and with support eventually all of the text. However the interaction is now one of an adult and a child and therefore in the context of a normal classroom the teacher will have organised the activities of the classroom in order for such one-to-one interactions to take place.

The shared reading which is suggested here is not unlike the apprenticeship approach suggested by Waterland (1985). In this approach Waterland argued that the adult would read with the child and each would contribute to the reading from the book, indeed there would be a gradual development from the child listening to the reading to the child reading alongside the teacher and then the child begins to take over the reading. None of this sequence can be prescribed however, there is a gradual move towards the child having a more prominent reading role although on occasions the emphasis might be altered and the teacher would again be the main reader. The teacher, sensitive to the needs of the child, will make decisions about how the learner can best be supported on any particular reading.

The key elements of shared reading are the book, the learner, the teacher and the collaboration that occurs during the interaction. Using these key elements a whole range of shared or paired reading activities have been suggested (Topping, 1986). In this variety of suggestions different roles for the teacher or the learner are suggested and the procedures of teacher reading first or of an initial combined reading might be noted. In some instances a more structured approach is suggested, e.g. reading of alternate pages by the adult and the child. However the key elements remain and Davis and Stubbs (1988a) emphasize these elements in a slightly different way. They suggest that the important features of shared reading are in the choice of story and parental involvement. The story to be read is chosen by the child from a selection of 'real' or meaningful books. That book will be shared with a parent. The parental involvement is encouraged in part because the quality of attention and time can only occur where support is given to the teacher but also in recognition of the major contribution to the child's literacy development that comes from such involvement (e.g. Hewison and Tizard, 1980).

Davis and Stubbs (1988b) suggest that what will occur in these shared readings will be some books read by the adult to the child, some shared and some read by the child to the adult. These procedures are not substantially different from the apprenticeship approach although Waterland (1985) does emphasize the word 'with'. Indeed she argues that it is the use of the word with and the associated change in the role of the teacher and the child that is crucial in this approach to encouraging reading development. Shared reading in the reading together continuum draws upon those ideas and might be defined as the interaction of an adult reading with a learner and encouraging and facilitating an increasingly more prominent reading role for the learner.

Of course during the process of shared reading the child's contribution to the reading will not always be an exact reading of the print. The meaning might be conveyed but the actual words spoken may vary from the text. However these emergent readings may be an important stage in the process towards more conventional readings (Teale, 1988). Furthermore Teale argues that story readings and perhaps repeated readings of the same book will encourage emergent readings and the move to more conventional processing of print. Shared reading extends this development and enables the child to produce emergent readings and, with the guidance and support of the teacher, move towards conventional reading.

In addition to the encouragement from emergent reading to a conventional reading what else does the learner gain from a shared reading interaction? Martin (1989) refers to a sharing of books between a reader and non-reader, albeit in the context of older children who have made a limited start with their reading, and argues the merits of such events. He notes that such sharings provide the learner with a model of the reading, it enables the learner to read like a fluent reader from the start and it gives the support to the learner so that getting stuck on words does not occur. Therefore during these early stages of development as a reader the learner's confidence can be built up.

And perhaps most importantly what shared reading provides is a pleasurable experience for the child. However, as Whitehead (1987) noted it is no less intellectually demanding because it is enjoyable. The teacher and the child are involved in a complex interaction. In particular the supportive role of the teacher is complex and subtle (Dombey, 1987). The teacher will mediate in the reading where required, tolerate restarts and meaningful miscues and generally provide the support necessary to facilitate the child's progress through the book. With such guidance the children will create their own understanding of the books that they share. And the books will be meaningful story books, because as Meek (1988) has shown the stories contained in such books have so much to teach the young child who is developing as a reader.

However, once again in order to try to clarify the debate on shared reading two examples of five-year-old children sharing a read with their teacher will be provided. In the first of these examples the teacher reads the story to the child and then Kirsty provides a reading of the story. In the second example the teacher and the child read the book together and then Robert reads the book to the teacher. Therefore across the two examples can be seen the gradual handing over of independence to the emergent and increasingly conventional reader (Whitehead, 1987). And although at certain points it is the teacher reading to the child and at other points it is the child reading to the teacher the impression created by the transcripts is of the teacher reading with the child. (An impression which is emphasized by the tapes where the intonations indicate the genuine sharing of the books.)

Shared reading: Kirsty and her teacher

This example is taken from a reception class of an infant school. Five-year-old Kirsty had selected a book to read with her teacher. The other children in the class were involved with the various activities of the infant classroom, e.g. painting, making, writing, play at the water table etc. Once Kirsty was settled by the side of the teacher then the teacher began the sharing.

Teacher: I wonder what Dizzy Dog is going to do?
Eh? Doesn't he look funny?
I'll read it to you first shall I?
The dog sees the box.

So even before the teacher began to read to Kirsty she had presented the main character of the story, Dizzy Dog, albeit briefly. Furthermore, the teacher made a comment about the dog and invited Kirsty to comment. However as Kirsty appeared to be reluctant, at this stage, to respond the teacher suggested that she would read the story to Kirsty. This suggestion indicated that there would be a real sharing with the teacher reading the book first. This short opening indicated a feature which Waterland (1985) suggested would be apparent; the teacher would be performing with the child rather than having as the objective listening to the child perform.

Teacher: Where's the box Kirsty?
Kirsty: Upstairs.
Teacher: It's upstairs.
         What's the dog going to do now?
Kirsty: Sniff.
Teacher: Yes.
         The dog sniffs the box.

Rather than continuing to read the teacher asked Kirsty another question in order to involve her in the sharing. The first question brought forth a response albeit a one word answer. The subsequent question required Kirsty to predict what might happen next. That prediction would be aided by the picture which was on that particular page. Kirsty's correct response was followed by the teacher reading the next sentence which acted as a confirmation to the response. These questions might have been used to encourage Kirsty's involvement with the book. And Kirsty demonstrated her involvement with her next initiated comment.

Kirsty: My dog does that.
Teacher: Does he?
Kirsty: When my dad first brought my rabbit.
Teacher: Does he?
         Now.
         The dog kicks the box.
Kirsty: [Laughs]
Teacher: That wasn't very good was it?
         Oh, What's he doing now?
Kirsty: Climbing in it.
Teacher: Yes.
         The dog gets in the box.
         Oh dear, and what's happened now?
Kirsty: Falling down the stairs.
Teacher: Yes, and who's in the box?
Kirsty: The dog.
Teacher: Yes.
         It's fallen all the way down the stairs – bump, bump, bump.
         Now.

> The dog gets out of the box.
> And what does he try to do?

Kirsty: Stand up.
Teacher: Yes.

> The dog falls

Kirsty: over.
Teacher: over.

> Yes.

As might be expected the teacher responded to the initiated comments from Kirsty, although it might be argued that on this occasion the teacher could have demonstrated the sharing more thoroughly by sustaining the dialogue rather than simply replying 'Does he?'. However, what is apparent is that Kirsty was enjoying the shared reading and she laughed at the story line as the teacher continued with the read. Furthermore the teacher also continued to ask questions about the story. Those questions were framed in ways which required more than a yes/no answer. Kirsty was being asked to predict the events of the story. All of these aspects served to keep Kirsty involved with the story rather than the teacher just reading the book and having Kirsty as a listener. In addition two other features of the interaction brought Kirsty closer to the story. First, the teacher highlighted the story with her 'bump, bump, bump' and second, the teacher used a rising intonation as she read 'The dog falls' and therefore invited Kirsty to contribute to the reading, which Kirsty did with success. The teacher then carried on with the reading of the book.

Teacher: The dog stands up.
But what happens?
Kirsty: He's too dizzy.
Teacher: Yes.

> The dog is dizzy.
> And he ends up being a
> Dizzy dog.

At that point in the sharing the teacher had read the complete story to Kirsty. She therefore invited Kirsty to read the story to her. Of course the words as they appear in this text 'Your turn to read it.' might suggest a command from the teacher to the child. However the intonation offered with the words suggest otherwise. The utterance was provided in a way which indicated a sharing of the story with both teacher and child able to read from the book.

Teacher: Would you like to read it to me now Kirsty?

	Your turn to read it.
	All right dear let's see.
Kirsty:	The dogs sees a [the] box.
Teacher:	Mmh.
Kirsty:	He [The dog] sniffs in the box.
Teacher:	He sniffs it doesn't he?
Kirsty:	He [The dog] kicks the box.
	He [The dog] climbs [gets] in the box.

Although Kirsty produced a number of miscues of substitution, 'a' (the), 'He' (The dog) three times and 'climbs' (gets) as well as inserting the word 'in', she did retain the meaning of the story and so the teacher made no comment about the miscues. Indeed after each of the first two sentences read by Kirsty the teacher provided some support for what had been read. The 'Mmh' served to sustain and encourage Kirsty in her reading and the 'He sniffs it doesn't he?' appeared to accept and confirm the use of 'He' for 'The dog'. The use of 'He' for 'The dog' after the first presentation of the character was quite appropriate and reflected what might be expected in many books. It might be argued that it demonstrated Kirsty's knowledge about the use of pronouns in a story. However, most importantly Kirsty was behaving like a reader and producing a meaningful story.

Teacher:	Oh, now what happens?
Kirsty:	He falls down the stairs.
	The dog falls [gets] out (of) the box.
	The//
Teacher:	The
Kirsty:	The dog falls over.

In the above short section the teacher asked a question about the story before Kirsty continued to read. Further 'good' miscues of 'falls' (gets) and the omission of 'of' were ignored by the teacher. She appeared to be following the dictum of Hood (1978) that miscues such as dialect variations or those which preserve the essential meaning of the text might receive no response from the teacher. However, Kirsty's hesitation was supported by the teacher. Quite simply she restarted the sentence and with a rising intonation invited Kirsty to continue with the reading. Despite what might appear to be a rather limited and simple support for the reader nevertheless it worked for Kirsty and she continued with her reading. A reading which the teacher confirmed with her next comment.

Teacher:	He does doesn't he?
	Then what does he try to do?

Kirsty: Stand up.
Teacher: And?
Kirsty: He's too dizzy   (The dog stands up.
               he can't stand up.   The dog is dizzy.)
Teacher: That's right.
           He's too dizzy he can't stand up.
           He ends up being a ?
Kirsty: Dizzy dog.
Teacher: A dizzy dog.

At the end of the book the text indicates that 'The dog stands up.' and 'The dog is dizzy.'. However, Kirsty's reading suggested a child-like perception of a dog that is dizzy being unable to stand up, a view which was to some extent encouraged by the pictures of these pages being read. The teacher confirmed Kirsty's view that a dizzy dog would not be able to stand. And, perhaps more importantly, the teacher confirmed that Kirsty's reading had been a valid retelling of the story.

Teacher: Did you enjoy that book?
           Why?
Kirsty: It's a funny one.
Teacher: It's a funny one.
Kirsty: My rabbit done that one day.
Teacher: Did he?
           What did he try to do?
Kirsty: He saw a box.
Teacher: Mmh.
Kirsty: The doors open and I lifted him in.
Teacher: Yes.
Kirsty: And he – and I pushed him.
           He fell all the way down stairs and bumped into the door.
Teacher: Did he, and was he all right? And did he get up, and what happened?
           He was?
Kirsty: He went outside and then fell over again.
Teacher: So he was dizzy just like Dizzy Dog.
           Well done Kirsty.

This shared reading lasted for just over three minutes and took place in a normal classroom setting. Therefore the teacher had other children in the class to attend to and to share a reading. Nevertheless she gave time to Kirsty at the end of the read in order to ask some questions about the story and about Kirsty's enjoyment of the book. The teacher also utilized the contribution from Kirsty about her own personal experiences with her rabbit and, therefore, demonstrated that this really was a genuine sharing in which the learner as well as the teacher could set the topic of conversation. The teacher concluded the shared reading by making a connection between Kirsty's telling of her personal experiences and the Dizzy Dog in the story, together with a final word of praise.

An important feature of the shared reading was that meaning and story line were considered to be more important than absolute word accuracy. This feature can be emphasized by noting the text and Kirsty's reading alongside each other.

Text	Kirsty
The dog sees the box.	The dog sees a box.
The dog sniffs the box.	He sniffs in the box.
The dog kicks the box.	He kicks the box.
The dog gets in the box.	He climbs in the box.
The dog gets out of the box.	The dog falls out the box.
The dog falls over	The dog falls over.
The dog stands up.	He's too dizzy he can't stand up.
The dog is dizzy.	
Dizzy dog	Dizzy dog.

If a simple system of counting the miscues was to be employed then Kirsty might be regarded as reading at a frustrational level rather than an instructional or independent level (Betts, 1946). And yet there was never a sense of that being the case. Kirsty appeared to be learning about reading, enjoying and learning to read. The emphasis upon meaning, the genuine sharing of the text, the relationships within the interaction and the guidance and support from the teacher contributed to making it a worthwhile literacy event for the young developing reader.

In the first chapter, the Smith (1978) dictum of needing to read in order to learn to read was noted. Shared reading provides the opportunity for this to occur. Kirsty was not yet able to read, at least in the form of conventional reading, but shared reading allowed her to read as part of the process of learning to read. With the support of the teacher Kirsty was indeed learning to read by reading.

Shared reading: Robert and his teacher

The second example is again taken from a reception class of an infant school. And once again the teacher had organized the classroom so that the children were engaged upon a variety of activities. This careful organization allowed the teacher to spend time upon individual interactions for various purposes. These purposes included shared readings with a number of the children.

Five-year-old Robert had also selected a book which he was going to share with his teacher. However, unlike Kirsty who had the book read to her before she read it to her teacher, Robert was perceived to be able to read the book alongside his teacher right from the start of the interaction. Then, after reading alongside his teacher, Robert read for a second time with less direct support from her. The interaction began as soon as Robert and his teacher were settled side by side with the book in front of them.

Robert:	I'm reading this book now.
Teacher:	That's it and what's it called?
Robert:	(I can) jump.
Teacher:	I can jump.
	Isn't it?
	That's a nice looking book.
Robert:	I can jump.
Teacher:	That's it.
Robert:	'I can jump,'
	said the//
Teacher:	grasshopper.
Robert:	grasshopper.
Teacher:	Can you see the grasshopper in that picture?
	There he is.
	He hops up high, doesn't he?

An immediate feature of this interaction was Robert's confident start, 'I'm reading this book now'. Robert perceived himself as a reader and was currently reading that particular book. As might be expected the teacher began to ask about the book. However, the first question about the title of the book led the teacher and Robert away from that discussion and into a reading of the text. In part this might have been because Robert miscued the title with an omission of 'I can'. Nevertheless the teacher supported Robert in his reading by reading the title and confirming with Robert that 'I can jump' was the title. Now although it could be argued that the teacher had corrected Robert in his reading, the flow of the dialogue suggests that it was more of a support and guidance to help Robert along with his reading rather than to correct for word accuracy.

Robert:	'I can(can't) jump,'
	said the
Teacher/Robert:	snail.

Teacher:	Mmh.
	He can't jump can he?
Robert:	He goes underneath.
Teacher:	Yes, they crawl along don't they?
Robert:	Yes.
	'I can jump(run),'
Teacher:	'I can run,'
Robert:	run,'
	said the spider.
Teacher:	said the spider.
Robert:	'I
Robert/Teacher:	can't run,'
Robert:	said the snail.
Teacher:	No, he can't run can he?
Robert:	He goes slow.
Teacher:	He just goes very slowly along the ground doesn't he?

As the shared reading continued there were occasions when the teacher and Robert were reading together from the book. However, a close listening to the recordings suggest that one of the pair was always fractionally in front. Thus the teacher guided Robert to read the word 'snail' on the line:

Teacher/Robert: snail.

In contrast Robert was leading the reading of 'can't run,' and supported by the teacher on the line:

Robert/Teacher: can't run,'

Both of these examples demonstrate how a real collaborative shared reading was taking place. Goodman (1986) suggested that children should read along with their teacher and take over the reading if they so choose. Robert was doing both in this example of a shared read. Because this was the case, the transcription of the interaction almost suggests that there was a somewhat disjointed reading of the book. However, the recording does not give that impression. Listening to the tape recording creates a sense of combined reading in which each person is contributing to the overall success of the literacy activity.

The combined or shared reading was emphasized by the teacher's support for Robert's reading of can/can't. The theme of the book is centred upon creatures that can/can't jump, run and fly. Therefore Robert had to read with some care each line in order to recreate the meanings of the book.

The teacher helped in that quest by supporting his reading rather than correcting in a very direct way the miscues that were produced. Thus when Robert first met the word 'can't' he miscued with 'can'. The teacher responded to the miscue indirectly with her comment 'He can't jump can he?' and then had a brief discussion with Robert about how the snail moved. The next sequence associated with the can/can't miscues produced:

Robert: 'I can jump(run),'
Teacher: 'I can run,'

The teacher confirmed the reading of 'can' as part of an utterance which also mediated in the use of the word 'jump' for the text word 'run'. Finally in this section of the shared reading 'can't' again appeared in the text:

Robert: 'I
Robert/Teacher: can't run,'
Robert: said the snail.
Teacher: No, he can't run can he?

In order to support Robert in his reading of 'can't' the teacher read alongside Robert. Reading alongside may have been particularly important because it was 'can't' in the text, rather than 'can', which was creating problems for Robert. Once Robert had completed the sentence the teacher confirmed the reading with her comment 'No, he can't can he?'

The exchanges between Robert and his teacher when meeting can/can't in the text demonstrate how the teacher attempted to support Robert in his reading. That support involved the use of different strategies but avoided the direct correction of Robert's miscues. The strategies employed by the teacher tended to emphasize the collaborative nature of the shared reading. The teacher worked alongside the reader in order to read with him rather than sitting in judgement of the miscues that were produced and correcting them directly. In this way the enjoyment of reading was maintained.

However, to return to the shared reading of the book, the teacher and Robert were now looking at the next page. The teacher invited Robert to continue with the reading by introducing the next character in the book:

Teacher: Oh, what does the butterfly think he can do?
Robert: 'I can fly,'
           said the butterfly.
Teacher: Yes.

Robert:	'I-I//
Teacher/Robert:	can't
Robert:	jump(fly),'
	said the snail.
Teacher:	Yes.
	Can you fly?
Robert:	No.
Teacher:	No, you can't.
	He looks a bit frightened there.
	Can you see him in the picture?
Robert:	He's opened his mouth.
Teacher:	He has opened his mouth hasn't he?
	That's right.
	'But
Teacher/Robert:	I can
Robert:	walk(slide).'
Teacher/Robert:	can slide.'
Robert:	Down the leaf.
Teacher:	Yes, do you like to slide?
	Where do you go for sliding?
Robert:	At the swings.
Teacher:	At the swings.
	And is there a big slide there or is it a little slide?
Robert:	A big slide.
Teacher:	A big slide.
	And how do you get up on to the top of the slide?
Robert:	I climb up the ladder.
Teacher:	Oh, you go up the ladder do you?
	Mmh.
	So you're just like the snail you can slide down can you?

As the shared reading continued the teacher again supported Robert by reading alongside him when 'can't' was met once more in the book. She also extended Robert's involvement in the book by asking questions about the story but also by relating the story to Robert's personal experiences. So having read about the snail sliding down the leaf she asked Robert about his sliding in the playground. That questioning about sliding allowed the teacher to mention sliding seven times and to get from Robert an utterance which included the use of the word 'slide'. And perhaps provided the support which encouraged Robert to read 'slide' appropriately later in the interaction, as we shall see in due course.

As the interaction continued the teacher asked Robert a series of questions which were drawn from the text and which asked about the three actions of the story.

Teacher:	Now, what about these other things?
	Can you fly?
Robert:	No.
Teacher:	No.
	Can you run?
Robert:	Yes.
Teacher:	You can run.
	And where abouts do you go running?
Robert:	Home.
Teacher:	You go running home do you?
	What at the end of the day?
	And what about in the playground?
Robert:	I run every day.
Teacher:	You run every day do you?
	And what about this one?
	Can you jump?
Robert:	Yes.
Teacher:	How high can you jump?
Robert:	Just a little bit.
Teacher:	Just a little bit.
Robert:	He jumps up a lot.
Teacher:	What, the grasshopper does?
Robert:	Yes.
Teacher:	He jumps all the time doesn't he?
	Shall we read this again because you read that very nicely.
	Let's read it just one last time shall we?

Following the series of questions the teacher invited Robert to read the book again. The words used, especially 'we' suggested that it would be a shared and collaborative read. However as we shall see this second read involved a more sustained read from Robert and less mediation and support from the teacher. The reader was taking over more of the reading. He was being encouraged along the path towards becoming a more independent reader.

Robert:	'I can jump,'
	said the grasshopper.
Teacher/Robert:	'I can't
Robert:	jump,'
	said the snail.
Teacher:	He can't can he?
	Now it's the spider's turn.
Robert:	'I can run,'

	said the spider.
	'I can-can't run,'
	said the snail.
Teacher:	Good boy.
	Yes that's right he can't run.
	Now it's the butterfly.
Robert:	'I can fly,'
	said the butterfly.
	'I can't//
Teacher:	fly,'
Robert:	fly,'
	said the snail.
Teacher:	No he can't fly can he?
	But what can he do?
Teacher/Robert:	'But
Robert:	I can slide.'
Teacher:	Yes, good boy Robert.
	That was nicely read wasn't it?
	Now you're going off to get another book, are you?

In Robert's second reading a number of points were in evidence. First, the teacher did continue to mediate and support Robert in his reading but mediation and support were less frequently offered and were less sustained when given. Robert was being encouraged to take a more prominent reading role in the interaction. Second, Robert's reading of the book was closer to a conventional reading of text, miscues were fewer and there was a self-correction by Robert of his miscue of 'can't'. Indeed if we return briefly to that particular word then the sequence of reading 'can't' during this second reading is of some interest. The word 'can't' appears three times and Robert's reading of the word was first, alongside his teacher, then miscued as 'can' but self-corrected to 'can't' and finally read accurately. Third, there was still an appearance of the teacher in support of the reader and guiding him through the text. The reading alongside Robert, the introduction of two of the characters and the providing of a word 'fly' following the hesitation were evidence of that support and guidance to facilitate the reading by Robert. At the end of the read the teacher praised Robert and at that point there might have been further discussion of the book. However perhaps with the pressure of having to help the other children in the classroom she finished at that point. And, of course, none of the examples in this book are given as examples of what should be done although they do give useful insights into ways of proceeding which can be analysed and evaluated leading to minor changes in teacher behaviour in the future.

The two examples of shared reading taken together indicate the way in which a teacher might wish to read to a child and then to have the child read the book in what might be an emergent reading in which meaning is maintained but word accuracy may be less evident. Later the teacher and the child might read a book together with the teacher's contribution alongside the reader drifting in and out of focus. The teacher supports and guides in order to reduce the support and guidance! Following such readings the child might be encouraged to take a more prominent reading role in the interaction and with an increasingly conventional read. And the aim is to help the child towards independent reading on his/her own.

Summary

Shared reading might involve the teacher reading to the child, reading alongside the child or of the child reading to the adult (Davis and Stubbs, 1988a). However, the overall emphasis is of the adult/teacher reading with the child (Waterland, 1985). The teacher fades out the support given as the child takes over the reading (Goodman, 1986).

Drawing from the interactional perspective the role of the teacher is to sustain, guide, support and facilitate the reading by the child (Dombey, 1987). A genuine sharing and collaboration will be evident in the interaction (Wells, 1985).

The child's initial contributions to the reading of the book might be more suggestive of emergent readings. These emergent readings will eventually give way to more conventional readings (Teale, 1988).

Shared reading demonstrates the way in which children, not yet able to read, are able to learn to read by reading (Smith, 1978).

The support from the teacher (Martin, 1989) and the books that are read (Meek, 1988) are such that provide an enjoyable experience for the child (Whitehead, 1987).

Eventually the teacher's support and guidance within a shared reading is very greatly reduced. That reduction is brought about because the young reader is taking an increasingly prominent role in the reading of the book. The child is becoming an independent reader. As the child becomes more of an independent reader the teacher's role becomes more that of a listener, but ready to guide and facilitate the reading from time to time when the child requires some support. Listening to a child read is traditionally known as 'Hearing Children Read' in British primary schools and it is that activity which will be considered in the next chapter.

CHAPTER 4

Hearing children read

Hearing a child read develops gradually out of shared reading. The difference may be found in the increased independence of the reader and therefore in the changed roles of the child and the teacher. The child will now read from the book without first listening to the teacher read the text and without having had a read alongside the teacher. The teacher will become more of a listener and provider of occasional support when the child miscues especially in those instances where the miscues detract from the meaning of the story. In addition the teacher will want to lead a discussion about the content of the book in order to extend the child's involvement with the story.

However, although there may be differences between shared reading and hearing children read there are more similarities. The interaction, like all the interactions of reading together, requires sensitive teaching (Butler and Clay, 1979). There is a need for the teacher to demonstrate real involvement with the child's reading. That involvement includes listening carefully to the child's reading, comparing any miscues with the text word, responding with minimal interruption to those miscues and maintaining a structure to the interaction for the benefit of the reader (Campbell, 1988a).

The main constituents of hearing children read remain the adult/teacher, the child and meaningful books (Meek, 1982). However, for these elements to come together in a worthwhile interaction the teacher, with a responsibility for a class, would first have to attend to the organization of the classroom. The children would be involved with various activities arranged by the teacher which would give her the opportunity to be involved in an individual interaction. Where this initial attention to organization is not given then, of course, there is a real danger that the listening to a child read might be interrupted by other children or the teacher having to attend to other events (Southgate *et al.*, 1981). Nevertheless in most classrooms the teacher will be aware of these needs

but this is not always possible

and will organize the classroom in order to provide a positive teaching event for the reader.

With a well organized classroom the teacher will be able to demonstrate to the reader that a genuine collaboration is taking place. Although the child may be producing most of the reading there will still be evidence of a shared activity. And there will be support for what the child is trying to achieve (Goodman, 1986). Given such a social relationship the child will from time to time interrupt his/her own reading in order to talk about the book and to give direct or indirect reactions to it (Bettelheim and Zelan, 1982). These interruptions by the child occur because the child feels secure within the interaction and feels that thoughts can be expressed to the teacher about what is being read. And this will be the case because the teacher will be sharing the book with an emphasis upon meaning, attending to the reader, allowing time for the interaction to be completed in a natural manner, and in general suggesting an empathy with the reader (Campbell, 1988).

Although the teacher will now be, in the main, a listener there will be occasions when a response to miscues will be required. A number of researchers have studied such responses and provided ways of describing the variety of strategies that are used by teachers (e.g. Allington, 1980; Campbell, 1981; Hoffman and Baker, 1981). These descriptions suggest a range of strategies from those with a meaning emphasis to those which emphasize the graphophonic cues of language. However, for the teacher following a whole language perspective and wishing to keep the child involved with the text it will be the meaning based strategies that will predominate. For instance, as has already been noted in the shared reading chapter, the teacher will often not respond to those miscues which retain the meaning of the story. Furthermore, where the teacher feels that the miscue does require attention, perhaps because meaning is not retained, the strategies that are employed will be those that create a minimal disruption for the child's reading. In addition the teacher's response will from time to time be offered in such a way as to encourage the reader towards positive problem-solving strategies (Campbell, 1988a). Of course, there is always the danger that in suggesting ways of proceeding that those suggestions might become part of some ritualized activity (Goodacre,nd). Or, as when commenting upon the writing process Graves (1984) noted that the enemy is orthodoxy. Suggestions are in danger of becoming rules. However, providing the teacher is attempting to work with what the child is trying to do such dangers can be minimized.

As well as responding to some of the miscues the teacher will also want to develop a discussion with the reader about aspects of the book that has been read (Southgate *et al.*, 1981). This discussion might be about the content of the book and the child's feelings towards it. The discussion might also include questions from the teacher about personal experiences, comprehension and Veatch (1978) argued, mechanical aspects. In particular the teacher might wish to relate the story to the child's own personal experiences, as we noted the teachers did in the shared reading examples. The use of comprehension questions might be used to extend the child's involvement with the story. Questions about mechanical aspects, e.g. a particular word in the text, will on occasions lead to an interesting debate, perhaps about the word in question but often extending beyond the initial questioning.

Of course it must be remembered that the purpose behind the activity of hearing children read, as it is for the other activities of the reading together sequence, is to create an interest in books and an enjoyment of reading. Each of the literacy events are leading the children, via that interest and enjoyment to independent silent reading. Therefore although it is possible to isolate aspects of the interaction for analysis and evaluation it is the overall shared enjoyment of a book which provides the basis for success (Meek, 1982).

The transcriptions of two interactions in which the teacher is hearing a child read will enable us to appreciate the nature of this shared enjoyment. The examples also enable us to consider some of the elements of the interaction such as the teacher response to miscues and the discussions about the book being read. In the first example Brian reads a story from a book containing a collection of stories. Although the collection is an extension reader of a reading scheme, Brian was reading from it because the stories were of interest, they were meaningful to him, they contained a story structure and he enjoyed them. Brian was only just moving into a more independent reading and as we shall see he produced quite a number of miscues. In contrast Leah is well advanced in her reading and her reading to the teacher is confident and with relatively few miscues.

Hearing children read: Brian and his teacher

Brian, at the time of the recording was six-years old. He was in a middle infants classroom with children of the same age. As in the shared reading examples, Brian had selected the story to read to his teacher, and the other children were involved in a range of curriculum activities.

The interaction starts with the teacher asking about the title of the story. And perhaps because Brian miscues the title, like Robert in the second shared reading example, the discussion was diverted to the title. Consequently Brian moved from that discussion directly into his reading of the story. Had he not miscued the title then perhaps there would have been more of a discussion about the content of the story.

Teacher:	What's your story called?
Brian:	No Ducks [Ducklings] for Breakfast.
Teacher:	Duck
Brian:	Duckling
Teacher:	Ducklings for Breakfast.
	What are ducklings?
Brian:	They're sort of little ducks.
Teacher:	Yes.
	They're baby ducks.
	That's right.
Brian:	Ducks in the mud!
	Ducks in the mud!
	Left–Left, right! Left, right! They walk
	down in – in [to] the pond.
	Quack! Quack! they go.
	Down they go into – in the water, under the weed.
	We need weed.
Teacher:	We do need weed for our frog.
Brian:	One of them had [has] some eggs. She had [has]
	six of them.
	Out comes [come] the ducklings, out of her [their]
	shells.
	The ducklings fall [follow]
Teacher:	No.
	The ducklings
Brian:	followed [follow] her down in –
	down to the pond.
	They are learning to go under water like the
	big mother [ducks]
Teacher:	big
Brian:	duck [ducks].
Teacher:	Yes.

Once started on his reading the teacher chose not to respond to those miscues which retained the meaning of the story. Thus 'in' (to), 'had' (has) miscued twice, 'comes' (come), and 'her' (their) were not mediated. The outcome of such non-response is minimal disruption to the reader's flow of reading. Indeed had those miscues received a direct response then the interaction might have become very disjointed.

However where the teacher perceived the miscues to be less meaningful then she responded in a way which guided Brian back to an appropriate reading. For both 'fall'(followed) and 'mother'(ducks) she restarted the sentence, or read some of the words in front of the miscued word, and with a rising intonation invited Brian to carry on the reading. The strategy referred to as a word cueing move by Campbell (1988a) does appear to be helpful to young readers. Perhaps it reminds the reader of the syntactic and semantic context and therefore guides them to a more appropriate reading. Interestingly it is similar to the strategy which Clay (1979) noted able readers adopted to self-correct miscues. The reader goes back into the sentence in order to pick up the contextual cues which will then assist in the reading of the word which might be creating a problem.

In front of the first of these word cueing strategies the teacher had added a soft 'no'. This negative feedback was given without any punitive intonation. The 'no' provides information to the reader about how his predictions are working out. The teacher is working as an information provider (Smith, 1971).

A further feature of this opening section of the interaction was Brian's comment to his teacher, 'We need weed'. In the classroom at that time was a frog that was being cared for by the children. The story, by making reference to 'weed', reminded Brian of the need to look after the frog. And he felt sufficiently comfortable in the shared literacy event to be able to comment upon his reaction to the story. The teacher accepted his response and expanded upon it, therefore confirming both what had been said by Brian and the acceptability of his saying it. The social relationships of this interaction (Bettelheim and Zelan, 1982) encouraged a shared enjoyment of the content.

Brian: A – A big greedy(ginger) cat was – is walking(waiting) by the pond.
I like ducks [ducklings] for breakfast, he
said [says]. I like
fat [fluffy]

Teacher: I like

Brian: funny – funny

No.

fluffy, little ducklings. I am going to have a good breakfast.
His tail is going for – from side to side. He is waiting to jump on the ducks [ducklings] when they come out of the water.
Quack! Quack! Come here! Come here,
ducklings! Look at – Look out for the greedy [ginger]
cat or he
will have you for breakfast.

In this section of the interaction the only miscue to receive any teacher mediation was 'fat'(fluffy). The teacher again used the word cueing strategy of restarting the sentence and reading up to the miscued word with a rising intonation which invited the reader to continue the reading. Brian responded by correcting 'fat' to 'funny' told himself that was not right 'No' and then read the word appropriately as 'fluffy'.

An interesting feature of this sequence of miscues and self-correction concerns the nature of the miscue. The miscue sequence was 'fat' – 'funny' – 'fluffy', so Brian produced a miscue with first letter similarity then corrected that to a miscue with first and last letter similarity together with a 'u' and a double letter in front of the last letter. The word being offered always had some graphophonic similarities with the text word and these similarities were extended with each attempt at the word. And yet this was in a class where the teacher made only occasional comments about the graphophonic features of words, rather than teaching directly about the graphophonic cue system of language. Brian was learning about features of language during the process of learning to read in a whole language environment. Furthermore although Brian may have been attempting to produce a word which more closely matched the text word he did so while retaining syntactic and semantic appropriateness. 'fat', 'funny' and 'fluffy' all maintained the essential story line of the book being read.

The other substitutions that were produced during Brian's reading received no teacher response. Two of these miscues 'ducks'(ducklings) twice, and 'said'(says) made little change to the story. However, it could be argued that 'greedy'(ginger) and 'walking'(waiting) did alter the story to some extent. The main emphasis of the story was not changed by these miscues but there were changes in the author's intentions by the acceptance of these miscues by the teacher. It might have been that she did not want to interrupt the flow of reading by drawing Brian's attention to the miscues as they were uttered. However, at the end of the page and before turning over that page to read the last two pages the teacher did discuss one of those miscues.

Teacher: Yes, he is a greedy cat – what colour – that word isn't really greedy.
It does begin with a /g/.
What colour do you think the cat might be?

Brian: Grey colour – I mean – well it's got yellow in it but it's sort of black.

Teacher: Yes, it's a?

Brian: Oh, I know – I know what it is.

Teacher: Do you?

Brian: Yes, but I don't know what the word means.

Teacher: What colour cat do you think?

Brian: Grey.
Teacher: Grey colour, are you sure.
Brian: Yes that's what I think.
Teacher: Ginger cat.
Brian: Oh.
Teacher: He could be greedy.
            Who's he after?
Brian: The ducklings.
Teacher: The ducklings
            Yes.
            What for?
Brian: I wondered why he was all yellow, because he's been eating the
            ducklings.
Teacher: Yes, ginger cat.
            That's the word ginger.

So the teacher commented upon the 'greedy'(ginger) miscue. But she did this by first confirming that 'he is a greedy cat' and then questioning about 'what colour'. She also made a brief comment to confirm the first letter of the word. And when the teacher decided to provide the word for Brian 'Ginger cat' she also, almost immediately softened that correction by agreeing 'He could be greedy.' Within the discussion the teacher's use of language indicated the collaborative nature of the interaction rather than suggesting a teacher sitting in judgement of a learner.

Brian: Here comes(come) the ducklings, left, right,
                left, right, over the mud.
                They – Come under my wings, she said(says). You will
                be all right there. Be quick, come and hide under my
                wings.
                The ducklings are running to hide under her
                wings.
                You will not catch them now, she said(says) to the
                ginger cat. Go home! Go home! You will not
                have my ducklings for breakfast if I can help it.
Teacher: Well done, that's lovely.

After the discussion about 'greedy'(ginger) Brian restarted his reading and read through to the end of the story. In this reading he made just three miscues, none of which 'comes'(come), and 'said'(says), twice, did the teacher consider required a response. And 'ginger' was read as 'ginger'.

At the end of the reading by Brian it might have been expected that there would have been a discussion about the characters in the story, the story line or Brian's interest in the story. However, and perhaps it was because of the discussion prior to the reading of the last two pages that the teacher decided to complete the interaction with some praise for the reading and to close the interaction at that point. Whatever was the case, Brian demonstrated that he was moving towards independent reading and doing so supported by a teacher emphasizing meaning. That emphasis upon meaning meant that 'good' miscues received no teacher response and there was therefore minimal disruption to the reader's involvement with the text. When the teacher did respond her use of the word cueing strategy also minimized any disruption. This strategy encouraged the reader to carry on reading and perhaps suggested a strategy for the reader to use when reading independently and silently for himself.

Hearing children read: Leah and her teacher

Although Leah was the same age as Brian, and was in a middle infants classroom with other six-year-olds, she had moved from shared reading to reading to her teacher some time previous to the recording of this interaction. Her reading was more confident, contained few miscues and included patterns of intonation which indicated her understanding of the story which she read to her teacher.

The teacher's role was now more that of an interested audience, albeit there were a few points where she mediated to guide Leah's reading when she miscued. However as there was a more fluent read this fluency provided the opportunity for the teacher to extend the discussion about the story. All of which was possible because as in the previous examples of shared reading/hearing children read the other children in the classroom were catered for by the prior organization of activities by the teacher.

The book that was to be read by Leah was a classroom favourite, Good-Night Owl (Hutchins, 1972). Once Leah was side by side with her teacher and ready to start the interaction, the teacher asked her about the content of the book.

Teacher:	So what is it about?
Leah:	Good-Night Owl.
Teacher:	Good-Night Owl.
	What's owl doing?
Leah:	Trying to sleep.
Teacher:	Is he?
	When is he trying to sleep?
Leah:	Mh, during the day.

Teacher: Is he?

And that's when he usually sleeps is it?

We'll have to find out.

[aside] Yes Chris you may.

Leah: Owl tried to sleep.

Teacher: Oh, where's he trying to sleep?

Leah: In the tree, in the hole in a tree.

Teacher: That's right.

He is isn't he?

At the start of the interaction then there were questions about the story and about the main character 'Owl' that the teacher asked of Leah. However it was perhaps two other features of the opening which need to be considered. In this example the teacher responded, with an aside, to another child in the class. Perhaps it is inevitable that no matter how well organized the classroom might be there will always be, from time to time, children who seek the guidance of their teacher. The teacher will wish to deal with such interruptions as quickly and as quietly as possible, and give her main attention to the child reading. Despite that aside this interaction, and the others that have been explored, were not spoilt by the teacher diverting her attention to other activities. Having invited children to read to and with them, the teachers responded by listening and sharing in the interaction.

The other feature which was noted concerned the teacher's immediate reaction to Leah's reading of the first sentence, 'Owl tried to sleep.' It might have been expected that the teacher would have encouraged the reader to carry on reading rather than stopping the flow of reading almost before that reading had got started. However, that sentence is the only writing on the first two pages of the book and the teacher probably wanted to set the scene of the story before encouraging Leah into the rest of the text.

Leah: The bees buzzed,

buzz, buzz,

and owl tried to sleep.

The squirrel cracked nuts,

crack(crunch) crack(crunch), crack crack

and owl tried to sleep.

The crows croaked,

//

Teacher: The crows croaked,

Leah: cuw(caw)

Teacher: That's right.

Come on then.

Leah:	cuw(caw) cuw(caw),
	and owl tried to sleep.
	The woodpecker pecked,
	rat-a-tat! rat-a-tat!
	and owl tried to sleep.
Teacher:	Oh dear, what's happening Leah?
Leah:	All the animals are there. Umh, the crows, the woodpeckers and the squirrel and the-uh-crows are making a noise.
Teacher:	Why are they making a noise do you think Leah?
Leah:	They want to disturb owl.
Teacher:	They want to?
	Do you think that's the reason or might there be another reason do you think Leah?
	No, we'll wait and see shall we?

In the above section Leah had a sustained read of four of the pages of the book. During this reading the teacher only responded once following Leah's hesitation in front of the word 'caw'. In order to support the reader the teacher restarted the sentence and read up to the word which was causing Leah some problem. Leah then read the word as 'cuw'. However the teacher accepted that word and guided Leah to continue with her reading. The other miscue of 'crack'(crunch) was also accepted by the teacher. In both instances the words offered by Leah were sufficiently close to the text word, and animal noise, for the teacher not to interrupt her reading.

Another brief discussion about the story took place after reading the four pages. Part of the teacher's questioning included a question which required the reader to reason. As well as What? and When? questions there were also Why? questions. This discussion was followed by a more sustained read by Leah.

Leah:	The starlings chittered,
	tweet-tweet(twit-twit) tweet-tweet(twit-twit)
	and owl tried to sleep.
	The jays screamed,
	ark ark,
	and owl tried to sleep.
	The cuckoo croaked(called)
Teacher:	The cuckoo
Leah:	called
	cuckoo cuckoo,
	and owl tried to sleep.
	The robin peeped,
	pip pip pip pip,

and owl tried to sleep.
The /s/-sparrows chirped,
cheep cheep,
and owl tried to sleep.
The doves cooed,
cooo(croo) cooo(croo),
and owl tried to sleep.

Teacher: Oh dear.

Leah: The bees buzzed, buzz buzz.
The squirrel cracked nuts,
crack(crunch) crack(crunch) crack.
The crows croaked, caw caw.
The woodpeckers pecked,
rat-a-tat! rat-a-tat!
The starlings chittered,
twit-twit, twit(twit)
The jay screamed, ark ark.
The cuckoo called,
cuckoo cuckoo.
The Robin peeped, pip pip pip.
The sparrows cheeped(chirped),
cheep cheep cheep.
The doves cooed, coo(croo) coo(croo),
and owl tried to sleep – and owl couldn't sleep.

Leah read seven pages of the book and her intonation and emphasis as she read indicated a real involvement with the content and in particular with the various characters of the story. Although Leah added some animal noises in her reading e.g. 'pip', 'crack', and 'cheep' and omitted others e.g. 'twit' there was no need for the teacher to mediate in order to get an accurate reading from Leah, to do so would have been pedantic. Neither was there a need to get the animal noises conforming to the text in every detail e.g. 'tweet'(twit), 'cooo'(croo), and 'crack'(crunch), indeed Leah self-corrected one of those miscues herself on the second reading, 'tweet' corrected to 'twit'. Leah was reading with understanding and feeling. The teacher only commented on the reading twice, once to restart a sentence and enable Leah to correct her miscue of 'croaked'(called) and the second occasion to indicate her listening to the story and her shared involvement with the reader.

An interesting feature at the end of this part of the interaction was Leah's reading of the last line. It was not unreasonable for Leah to expect that the line would read 'and owl tried to sleep.' after all this was a constant theme of the book. However as she read the line in that way she was

Leah:	cuw(caw) cuw(caw),
	and owl tried to sleep.
	The woodpecker pecked,
	rat-a-tat! rat-a-tat!
	and owl tried to sleep.
Teacher:	Oh dear, what's happening Leah?
Leah:	All the animals are there. Umh, the crows, the woodpeckers and the squirrel and the-uh-crows are making a noise.
Teacher:	Why are they making a noise do you think Leah?
Leah:	They want to disturb owl.
Teacher:	They want to?
	Do you think that's the reason or might there be another reason do you think Leah?
	No, we'll wait and see shall we?

In the above section Leah had a sustained read of four of the pages of the book. During this reading the teacher only responded once following Leah's hesitation in front of the word 'caw'. In order to support the reader the teacher restarted the sentence and read up to the word which was causing Leah some problem. Leah then read the word as 'cuw'. However the teacher accepted that word and guided Leah to continue with her reading. The other miscue of 'crack'(crunch) was also accepted by the teacher. In both instances the words offered by Leah were sufficiently close to the text word, and animal noise, for the teacher not to interrupt her reading.

Another brief discussion about the story took place after reading the four pages. Part of the teacher's questioning included a question which required the reader to reason. As well as What? and When? questions there were also Why? questions. This discussion was followed by a more sustained read by Leah.

Leah:	The starlings chittered,
	tweet-tweet(twit-twit) tweet-tweet(twit-twit)
	and owl tried to sleep.
	The jays screamed,
	ark ark,
	and owl tried to sleep.
	The cuckoo croaked(called)
Teacher:	The cuckoo
Leah:	called
	cuckoo cuckoo,
	and owl tried to sleep.
	The robin peeped,
	pip pip pip pip,

Teacher: Oh dear.

and owl tried to sleep.
The /s/-sparrows chirped,
cheep cheep,
and owl tried to sleep.
The doves cooed,
cooo(croo) cooo(croo),
and owl tried to sleep.

Leah:

The bees buzzed, buzz buzz.
The squirrel cracked nuts,
crack(crunch) crack(crunch) crack.
The crows croaked, caw caw.
The woodpeckers pecked,
rat-a-tat! rat-a-tat!
The starlings chittered,
twit-twit, twit twit.
The jay screamed, ark ark.
The cuckoo called,
cuckoo cuckoo.
The Robin peeped, pip pip pip.
The sparrows cheeped(chirped),
cheep cheep cheep.
The doves cooed, coo(croo) coo(croo),
and owl tried to sleep – and owl couldn't sleep.

Leah read seven pages of the book and her intonation and emphasis as she read indicated a real involvement with the content and in particular with the various characters of the story. Although Leah added some animal noises in her reading e.g. 'pip', 'crack', and 'cheep' and omitted others e.g. 'twit' there was no need for the teacher to mediate in order to get an accurate reading from Leah, to do so would have been pedantic. Neither was there a need to get the animal noises conforming to the text in every detail e.g. 'tweet'(twit), 'cooo'(croo), and 'crack'(crunch), indeed Leah self-corrected one of those miscues herself on the second reading, 'tweet' corrected to 'twit'. Leah was reading with understanding and feeling. The teacher only commented on the reading twice, once to restart a sentence and enable Leah to correct her miscue of 'croaked'(called) and the second occasion to indicate her listening to the story and her shared involvement with the reader.

An interesting feature at the end of this part of the interaction was Leah's reading of the last line. It was not unreasonable for Leah to expect that the line would read 'and owl tried to sleep.' after all this was a constant theme of the book. However as she read the line in that way she was confronted with text words which did not exactly meet her expectations, she therefore self-corrected to 'and owl couldn't sleep'. This self-correction demonstrated Leah's emphasis upon meaning in her reading and how the teacher's empathy for what the reader was trying to achieve, including not responding to 'good' miscues, supported and facilitated that development as a meaningful reader.

The teacher supported Leah, following her self-correction, and then asked her a question – Why?

Teacher:	No, he couldn't.
	Why couldn't he sleep?
Leah:	Because they were all making a noise.
Teacher:	Why do you think they were all making a noise?
	Mmh?
Leah:	Because it's still-umh . . .
Teacher:	In when?
Leah:	Because it's not night yet.
Teacher:	It isn't night time.
	And what do owls do at night time?
Leah:	They – They don't – umh – They don't sleep in night and they wake up and – and they...
Teacher:	Yes and what do they do at night?
Leah:	Sleep – no wake all the others up.
Teacher:	Yes, that's right.
	So when do they try to sleep?
Leah:	In the nights – umh – in the day.
Teacher:	That's right, in the day time.

Therefore the discussion first supported Leah's self-correction to 'and owl couldn't sleep' and then debated the theme of the story. In that debate Leah made a number of hesitant starts but always corrected herself and provided accurate interpretations of the story. The teacher waited for the reader to think through the answers and produce the corrected response. In this discussion, as in the reading from the book, the teacher was giving the learner time to reason and to construct her own meanings from the book.

The teacher then invited Leah to continue with her reading of the last two pages and the resolution of the story.

Teacher:	And now what happens?
Leah:	Then dark(darkness) fell
	and the middle(moon)
Teacher:	and the

Leah:	the moon came up.
	And the – there was (wasn't) a
Teacher:	And there
Leah:	there was – wasn't a sound.
	Owl screamed(screeched)
	screech screech,
	and owl(woke) – and wakes(woke) everyone up.
Teacher:	Oh yes, he woke everyone up didn't he?

Perhaps because the rhythm of the story alters at this point Leah produced a greater proportion of miscues on the last pages of the book. Two of these miscues 'dark'(darkness) and 'screamed'(screeched) received no response from the teacher. The reader was maintaining the meaning of the text and there was no need for the teacher to mediate, which at that point would have been to have caused a disruption to the reader's involvement with the book. And a key feature of the whole language teacher at work would be to allow the young reader to remain actively involved with the book.

However, the teacher did respond to the miscues of 'middle'(moon) and 'was'(wasn't), both of which did have an effect upon the meaning within the story. Nevertheless the teacher responded in a way which produced very little disruption, kept the reader involved with the text, requested the reader to reconsider the text and maintained a flow in the reading. The teacher had once again used the simple, but effective strategy, of reading some of the words leading up to the miscue.

The final substitution from Leah, 'owl'(woke) corrected to 'wakes'(woke) did not receive a teacher response. However the teacher both confirmed and corrected the miscue with her immediate comment of 'Oh yes, he woke everyone up, didn't he?'

Overall there was an impression of the teacher supporting and guiding Leah in her development as an independent reader. Yet, the teacher kept in the background while Leah was reading. (A feature which can be contrasted with the teachers in the shared reading examples where a more prominent role was adopted by the teachers, albeit as a stage towards reducing that prominence.) The support indicated to the reader the importance of meaning and any response to miscues were simple and short in order to encourage the reader to continue to actively and constructively interact with the language of the book.

At the conclusion of the read the teacher followed her brief comment upon the 'wakes'(woke) miscue by asking Leah about her enjoyment of the book.

Teacher: Did you enjoy that book? You did? Why did you?

Leah:	'Cos –'Cos the other – the other animals was making all noises and then when darkness fell he were calling the other animals up.
Teacher:	He did. Why did – What did he want to do?
Leah:	Go to sleep in the day.
Teacher:	He wanted to sleep in the day, but what did he want to do during the night time?
Leah:	Wake all the other animals up.
Teacher:	And do what?
Leah:	Hunt.
Teacher:	And?
Leah:	For food.
Teacher:	For food. Good girl, Leah. Well done. Thank you, off you go.

Leah had already demonstrated her involvement with and understanding of the book during the time that she had been reading. She emphasized this understanding in the short discussion with the teacher which brought the interaction to an end. And the teacher structured the last few comments in order to conclude the interaction in a manner which suggested to the reader the importance of her contribution. The teacher appeared to have time to spare for Leah and yet there were other children to attend to in the classroom. An important part of reading together may be for the teacher to demonstrate the availability of time for the reader despite the inevitable pressures of caring for all the children in the classroom.

The teacher will also have demonstrated to the reader that a genuine sharing of the book is an important aspect of the interaction. In part this sharing is emphasized by the nature of the responses that are provided by the teacher following the reader's miscues. These teacher responses have been noted during the discussion of the interactions that have been provided. However it may be useful to consider these responses, and the principles that might govern their use, as a separate section.

The teacher response to miscues

Although the teacher will use a number of strategies in order to support and guide the child in his/her reading of the text it will have been apparent from the interactions which have been explored that certain strategies predominate. In particular four different teacher responses appeared with some frequency. These teacher responses included:

Non-response: the teacher decides not to mediate, e.g.

Brian: One of them had(has) some eggs. She had(has) six of them.

Out comes(come) the ducklings, out of her(their) shells.

Teacher: ____

As has already been noted the teacher response to the miscues of 'had'(has) miscued twice, 'comes'(come), and 'her'(their) was to not respond. Non-response is regarded as a teacher response because it is a carefully considered and deliberated decision taken by the teacher. In the above example the miscues did little to alter the meaning of the story. The teacher therefore chose not to respond to the miscues. If each of the miscues had received an overt response then the outcome would have been a disjointed read produced by Brian. The teacher's emphasis upon meaningful reading suggests that a non-response to miscues which retain the story meanings would be appropriate.

Word cueing: the teacher reads part or all of the sentence leading up to the miscue but not the miscued word. A rising intonation indicates that a question is being asked, namely what is the next word, e.g.

Leah: The jays screamed,
ark, ark,
and owl tried to sleep.
The cuckoo croaked(called)

Teacher: The cuckoo
                    called
cuckoo, cuckoo,
and owl tried to sleep.

This simple strategy seems to work, as it did in the above example. It is a strategy which does not disrupt the reader's involvement with the book being read. The teacher only uses words that are part of the text and which have already been read by the child. The use of this strategy therefore appears to emphasize the sharing of the book.

One of the reasons why this teacher response to a miscue might be successful is that it reminds the reader of the contextual cues. Both the sentence structure and the meaning is emphasized by the teacher's reading of part of the sentence. And because the teacher only uses the words of the text it encourages the child to remain actively and constructively involved with the book.

Furthermore the response by the teacher is similar to the strategy which Clay (1979) noted that some able readers adopted in order to self-correct their own miscues. By using this response the teacher is perhaps encouraging the reader to develop positive reading strategies which might be used on future occasions (Campbell, 1988a).

Negative feedback: the teacher makes a negative comment to indicate that a word has been miscued, e.g.

Brian:	The ducklings fall (follow)
Teacher:	No.
	The ducklings
Brian:	followed(follow) her down in –
	down to the pond.

In this example the teacher provided both negative feedback 'No' and a word cueing strategy 'The ducklings'. However at other times the teacher will respond to the child's miscue with just the negative feedback. Often this will be at the beginning of the sentence and especially where the first word of the sentence is miscued. In such circumstances the use of a word cueing strategy is denied to the teacher and a soft 'No' might be given.

The 'no' is soft because it is provided as a source of information and not as a punishment for an incorrect reading. As Smith (1971) suggested the negative feedback is given without any punitive intonation. The intention is to make the reader aware as to how his/her attempts at reading are working out.

This teacher response, like the previous responses, provides a minimal disruption to the child's involvement with the book being read. Few words are used and the reader is not distracted from the text. Instead the soft 'no' provides a guidance to help the reader in the task.

Provide the word: the teacher provides the miscued word for the reader, e.g.

Robert:	'I can jump(run),'
Teacher:	'I can run,'
Robert:	run,'
	said the spider.

In this extract the teacher simply provides the word for the reader and he then echoes the teacher's response and carries on reading. Not surprisingly this example is taken from the shared reading chapter. In general a teacher will provide the word for a younger and early beginning reader more frequently than for a reader who is becoming more independent in his/her reading. The strategy helps the reader maintain a link with the text and it also demonstrates to the reader that the reading together is a genuine shared experience.

The response of providing the word may also be used at the start of a sentence where other responses may be less applicable. A feature of this response, like the other responses already discussed, is that it does not distract the reader from the text. However, an over use of providing the word may lead children to expect the answer if they wait long enough. This response would, Yetta Goodman (1970) argued, hinder the child's attempt to discover reading strategies; it may also discourage self-correction. A problem with this strategy is that it makes less demand upon the child to remain as an active learner.

Of course the teacher will use other strategies in response to miscues and on occasions combine the responses, e.g. negative feedback and word cueing. However, these four simple responses will be observed frequently of a whole language teacher as the teacher attempts to guide and facilitate the young reader towards greater independence as a reader.

Why should these responses be predominant? First, each of the responses create a minimal distraction of the reader's involvement with the text. In addition the teacher provides information or reminds the reader about information that he/she already has. And the responses suggest strategies, albeit implicitly, that the reader might use in the future. The responses do attempt to keep the child as an active learner constructively making sense of the language of the book. All of the responses are provided within an atmosphere which encourages a shared enjoyment of books.

Summary

Hearing a child develops from shared reading as the reader gains greater independence as a reader. However, the interaction, like other literacy events, still requires sensitive teaching (Butler and Clay, 1979).

If the interaction occurs in a normal classroom setting the teacher needs to provide an organization that permits worthwhile interactions to occur (Campbell, 1988a). Without careful attention to classroom organization there may be frequent interruptions to the teacher/learner (Southgate *et al.*, 1981).

In a well-organized classroom the teacher will be able to provide a worthwhile literacy event in which the teacher will give support for what the child is trying to achieve (Goodman, 1986). Part of that support will demonstrate to the learner that the social relationship allows him/her to initiate questions about the book and to provide comments about it (Bettelheim and Zelan, 1982).

The teacher will respond to the miscues of the reader with a variety of strategies. Amongst those noted were non-response, word cueing, negative feedback and providing the word. However, what all these strategies emphasize is a minimal disruption of the reader in his/her involvement with the text. The strategies serve to encourage the child to remain as an active learner who constructs meaning from the book. Some of the teacher responses provide information for the learner and suggest strategies that the learner might use subsequently (Campbell, 1988a).

The teacher will discuss the book with the reader and relate the book to the child's personal experiences (Veatch, 1978). Such discussions will often occur before and after the reading takes place and occasionally within the read at appropriate points which serve to support the reader.

Nevertheless a shared enjoyment of the book remains an important objective (Meek, 1982). And this shared enjoyment encourages the young learner towards independent and silent reading. The next chapter will explore the notion of sustained silent reading as a continuation of the reading together sequence.

CHAPTER 5

Sustained silent reading

Reading together is provided in order to encourage children through the process of learning to read. And during this process to develop an enjoyment of books. Arising out of this enjoyment of books will be the motivation to read silently to oneself. For many children home will be where this silent reading will take place. However, for some children there may be many distractions at home (Fenwick, 1988). Therefore it becomes important to ensure that the children have opportunities to engage in silent reading at school. Furthermore there is a need to see that these opportunities for silent reading allow for a sustained read. There is some evidence to suggest that children's silent reading in schools may be in short bursts (Lunzer and Gardner, 1979) or limited in length (Southgate *et al.*, 1981) if the teacher in the classroom does not organize the classroom for a period of sustained silent reading. However, even though the children will be reading silently, a book of their own choice, it is still important for the teacher to be reading together with the children. Of course the role of the teacher will have altered and during sustained silent reading the teacher will be acting as a role model for the younger developing readers. Nevertheless as in the other literacy activities of reading together the teacher will still be functioning as a guiding adult working alongside and together with the learners.

In England it may have been the influence of the Extending Beginning Reading Report (Southgate, *et al.*, 1981) which created an impetus towards the use of sustained silent reading in primary classrooms. Certainly one of the major recommendations of that report was that more opportunities should be provided in the Junior school for personal reading by the children. Thus it was suggested that time should be set aside for regular and increasingly lengthy periods when every child in the class would read in a quiet atmosphere and without interruptions. Therefore it was not considered to be sufficient for that reading to occur while the teacher was involved with the register or other non-reading tasks. Indeed there is now some evidence which indicates that where sustained silent reading is provided during registration periods many children will be distracted from their reading and some children may do no reading at all (Mangan, 1988). The registration period was not the only period seen as inadequate by Southgate, *et al.*, (1981). Personal reading after the early completion of previously set tasks, although useful for some children, would not cater for all the children. Therefore a classroom in which a set time was allocated for sustained silent reading was suggested. And a number of key points were provided as guidance to help to establish the practice. Amongst these were: set aside a particular period every day for personal reading: ensure that every child has a personally selected book at an appropriate level; inform the children that they will have, say, 10 minutes to enjoy their books uninterrupted; the teacher sits at her/his own desk and also reads; every effort is made to ensure no talking or movement from chairs during this period and perhaps a 'do not disturb' notice will be placed on the classroom door; the time devoted to this personal, uninterrupted reading is gradually increased.

Of course the guidelines suggested above were not new and it is evident that they were in part drawn from a list given by McCracken (1971). In this earlier listing the view was expressed that there should be absolutely no reports or records of any kind, at least initially. The aim was to encourage children to read and not to spoil that enjoyment with the thought of reports to be written or records to be maintained.

In the McCracken article the acronym SSR (Sustained Silent Reading) was put forward although it was recognized that SSR had evolved from USSR (Uninterrupted Sustained Silent Reading) which had been suggested by Hunt (1970). Subsequently a whole range of acronyms have emerged. Bowermaster (1986) noted the use of SQUIRT (Sustained Quiet Uninterrupted Independent/Individualised Reading Time) and DEAR (Drop Everything And Read). In addition an example of a school using ERIC (Everyone Reading In Class) is explored later in this chapter and Fenwick (1988) makes reference to HIP (High Intensity Practice). To add to the confusion the acronyms do not always support the same words; ERIC has been used for Enjoy Reading In Class and SQUIRT has been used with a rather more forceful Stay Quiet You/U It's Reading Time. Nevertheless, although the list of acronyms continues to grow, more importantly, the message remains clear. SSR provides each learner with an uninterrupted period during which material of the learner's choice can be read silently (Allington, 1975). However, although sustained silent reading is simple in its concept, nevertheless like story reading, shared reading and hearing children read which precedes it, simplicity does not guarantee success. A sustained silent reading period requires careful organization and sensitive guidance from the teacher.

The adult/teacher, the child and interesting, meaningful books remain, as they were for the other elements of reading together, the key features. The teacher and the learners together share the pleasurable activity of silent reading. Indeed it is silent and independent reading that has been the goal of the earlier literacy activities. Of course, sustained silent reading can be imposed upon a class by a forceful teacher. However, what is required is a genuine sharing in which all the participants are involved in an enjoyable read and in which a pleasant atmosphere prevails. In part this pleasant atmosphere will be engendered by the relationships established in other reading together literacy activities. However, it will also be encouraged by the attention to organization that the teacher provides at this point. Three key aspects of this organization are concerned with time, materials and guidelines. Each of these aspects need to be considered (Campbell, 1988b).

Time is an important aspect of the sustained silent reading organization and there are two features which require attention. First, there is the time of day when sustained silent reading will occur. Ideally a period of time will be set aside each day for personal reading by all the children in the class – or even the whole school. A favoured period would seem to be either directly before the lunch break or immediately after lunch. Other times might be considered but the link to a natural break in the school day does appear to be appropriate. Whatever time is set aside for silent reading the teacher will have chosen that time because it seems to provide the best opportunity for quiet and settled conditions which will help to give the pleasant atmosphere for an enjoyable read by all the participants.

The other feature of time requiring attention concerns the length of time that will be devoted to silent reading. Of course this will be to some extent determined by the age of the children and the teacher's knowledge about their capabilities. For the youngest children in school 5 minutes might be suitable, for older children it might be 30 minutes. However, whatever time is reached eventually it is useful to start sustained silent reading with a very short period of time and gradually extend the time devoted to the activity over a number of weeks as the children become accustomed to the event. McCracken (1971) suggested that the children should be informed how much time they would have for reading but that a wall clock should not be used to time the session. The danger, McCracken argued, was that some children might become clock watchers. For this reason a desk timer was suggested. Many teachers who have used sustained silent reading with some success report that it is not clock watching that is a problem, getting the children to stop reading can be!

A second major feature of the organization for sustained silent reading concerns the materials to be read. Of course the materials to be read are selected by the children but the range of materials will have been determined, in the main, by the teacher when organizing the classroom. The predominant material will be books but both McCracken (1971) and Gambrell (1978) suggested that newspapers and magazines might also be used whereas the Extending Beginning Reading Report emphasized the use of books during the activity. Interestingly McCracken argued that no book changing should be permitted during sustained silent reading in order to encourage silence, however the Extending Beginning Reading Report suggested that the reader should have selected a second book, and have it to hand, if the first selected book was nearly completed. And if the object is to encourage reading then having an extra book readily available would seem to make sense. What is evident within schools that are using sustained silent reading is the need for a wide range of reading material which is readily accessible to the children. The teacher may shape the choice of books by the prior selection of books made available in the classroom, but the children make their own choice from that selection.

Although we have already noted a number of key points which provided some guidance to help to establish sustained silent reading there is also the need to provide guidelines for the operation of the activity in the classroom. These guidelines are mainly for young learners however they also are for others in the classroom. A simple rule of sustained silent reading is that during the activity there will be silence. Fenwick (1988) suggests that quietness rather than silence might be a more reasonable expectation for all ages but especially for the youngest children many of whom will still be reading orally for part of the time even when they are reading to themselves. In order to achieve the silence/quietness, movement around the classroom and interruptions are discouraged. A notice on the door to indicate that the class is reading – please do not disturb – might be used. And the children are encouraged to read silently. Part of this encouragement is derived from the second guideline; the teacher also reads. Indeed the importance of the teacher providing a model of silent reading is stressed constantly (Bergland and Johns, 1983). McCracken and McCracken (1978) go as far as to indicate that sustained silent reading will not work unless the teacher and any other adults in the room are reading. And the idea of the teacher also reading fits well with the philosophy of reading together. The children may be reading to themselves but the teacher is sharing that reading and is reading alongside the learner. Therefore the children are able to observe their teacher, and other adults in the room, demonstrating an interest in and enjoyment of reading. A further guideline for the children is that they are made aware that no reports or records of any kind are required of them. This is a time to enjoy reading it is not a preparation for some work in the future. Of course, a feature of sustained silent reading is that children will often want to tell about what they have read, as may the teacher. Such spontaneous reporting is welcomed but no formal report is required.

The above guidelines are set, not to create restrictions, but rather to provide the setting for a worthwhile session of reading. The objective is that all the readers in the classroom will be able to enjoy reading a book which is of interest to them. Of course demonstrating clearly that sustained silent reading is an effective use of school time can be problematic. Fenwick (1988) suggested that this literacy activity might lead to improvements in terms of the learners reading ability, attitudes towards reading and reading habits. Bowermaster (1986) provided some limited evidence (based on the work of Ekwall) of gains in reading performance following a year of sustained silent reading. Other evidence is mainly subjective, but nevertheless worthwhile. Teachers have suggested that sustained silent reading encourages the pupils to perceive reading as important. The learners will also perceive that books are meant to be read in large sections rather than as they learn throughout much of the school day that reading is carried out in short bursts. And importantly, as we shall note in some examples that are provided later, learners have commented favourably upon the enjoyment that they get from silent reading periods in the classroom.

The practice of sustained silent reading inevitably will vary according to the age of the learners. The use of the activity within the infant classroom is a possibility and Hong (1981) and Kaisen (1987) have suggested some adaptations that might be required with the younger children. Amongst those suggestions were that the teacher might work with a group within a class rather than a whole class; and that a much shorter time might be devoted to the activity. Junior classrooms are obvious venues for sustained silent reading. Most of the children will be well advanced, at seven to eleven years of age, towards silent and independent reading. Therefore the opportunity to engage in sustained reading periods will be appropriate. The Extending Beginning Reading Report did recommend the activity for this age group. And of course although the children at this age will still enjoy a story reading and some may still be sharing a read with their teacher or reading to their teacher, the predominant reading together activity at this stage will be silent reading. The activity will also be evident in the secondary school and Fenwick (1988) provides some details of the way it might be arranged in such schools. In particular the advantage of a whole school approach is debated.

In previous chapters the activities of reading together have been exemplified with the use of extracts from the language interactions in the classrooms. Clearly this is not possible in the case of sustained silent reading. However, it is possible to comment upon the attempts of two schools which endevoured to encourage reading through the use of sustained silent reading. Both of the schools are junior schools and in each case as well as describing the organization and conduct of sustained silent reading some comments, oral or written, by the children are provided.

Sustained silent reading: SQUIRT

One small four class junior school had set a time aside for SQUIRT, which meant for them Sustained Quiet Uninterrupted Independent Reading Time. In this school the activity occurs in the period immediately before the time when the school comes together for an assembly which in itself precedes the morning break. Although originally starting with a 10 minute allocation, the amount of time had gradually been increased to the point where SQUIRT lasted for 30 minutes on three mornings a week. The whole school was involved. Indeed the whole school came together, with a few exceptions, for the activity. The children came from each of the four classrooms into the dining hall with a book already selected from the classroom. Falling rolls had ensured that there was adequate space for this to be possible. Furthermore the large dining hall with posters/paintings on the walls provided a pleasant setting for the event. The children sat at a table, as did the headteacher who provided a sustained silent reading model, and read their chosen book. In some instances two books would be brought to the dining hall if one book was likely to be completed. When observed by the author the children appeared to be enjoying the activity and were very much involved in reading.

Although the majority of children read silently in the dining hall, small groups of children remained in their own classroom with their class teacher. In some instances these children in their own classroom would be involved with a sustained silent read but at other times they might be engaged in group reading with the teacher or individually reading to the teacher while others read silently. Thus while most children were involved with sustained silent reading some children had a shared reading or a hearing children read interaction with their teacher. The time in the classroom might also be used for such activities as group discussion of a text. Because there were only a few children left in the classroom with a teacher there was inevitably more time available for adult support and guidance. Of course, care had to be taken in the selection of children to remain with the teacher. If less able readers always stayed with the teacher then a danger of labelling might occur. This did not appear to be the case. And one of the children added some confirmation of that view;

> Some stay to read to teacher, they all have a turn to read, and some go to read in the hall. (Kathryn)

SQUIRT had been organized within the school partly to provide a stimulus for reading but also to provide each teacher with some time to give individual or group support to children as readers. In this sense the activity would appear to have been successful. However, it also gave the children the quiet setting to devote some time to a sustained read. And this purpose also appeared to be met;

> I never usually read myself but this is the one time that I get to read. (Jamie)

Certainly more time was being devoted to reading by the children than might otherwise be the case;

> It gives you enough time to read. (Yvette)

And in addition there was a feeling among the staff that this increased reading was providing more ideas for the children's writing.

Two important features of SQUIRT in this school were, first, the perceived need for the adult to provide a model of silent reading and second, to link the activity to a natural break in the school day. It was a strongly held view that the teacher, in this case the headteacher, should be a part of the sustained silent reading. Therefore the adult read at the same time as the learners. On some occasions the headteacher had, at the end of the activity, shared some of the text with the children by reading from the book and/or telling about what had been read. A development from this sharing by the adult was that some children would want to report about their books at the end of each session. McCracken (1971) had suggested that children would want to talk about the books they had read and, unless the teacher prevented it, would so so spontaneously. In this school the adult encouraged such reporting by demonstrating her own enthusiasm for and interest in books by commenting upon her reading. In other words the notion of sharing within reading together was maintained during sustained silent reading.

Also it was regarded as crucial that the activity was linked to a natural break in the school day. The session did not disrupt other school activities, nor was it disrupted by them, instead it fitted in well with the natural rhythms of the school day. This helped to create a relaxed and pleasant atmosphere for the sustained reading.

And perhaps most importantly, arising out of these two features, there was the sense of a genuine sharing of the pleasurable activity of reading. The learners and the teachers appeared to enjoy reading.

Sustained silent reading: ERIC

At another junior school a policy of ERIC (Everyone Reading In Class) had been adopted. The starting point for the activity had been the use by a few teachers of a 10 minute silent reading period in their classrooms. Of course, when only a few classes in the school were involved there was a need for a note on the door, of those classes, with requests not to disturb the class. And there had to be an agreement that such notices would be observed by everyone. However, with the apparent success of ERIC the activity had spread to all the classes in the school and therefore the notion of no movement/interruptions throughout the school was accepted fully;

> When we have ERIC time everybody is quiet. There is silence through the school. (Alex)

In each class the children selected a book and read in their own classroom with the teacher also reading during that time. Here too the view of the teacher reading as a key to success was argued by the teachers. The ERIC time was again linked to a natural break, with the last 10 minutes before lunch time being used on each school day. In some of the third and fourth year classes (nine to eleven years of age) ERIC was beginning to be started earlier in order to give a longer reading time and this would appear to be appreciated by the children although some suggested that even longer periods might be devoted to sustained silent reading;

> I look forward to ERIC but I think it should be half an hour because 15 minutes isn't really enough. (David)

From its beginning with a few teachers in the school ERIC had become part of the school policy in an attempt to provide all of the children with some personal time to read quietly. It was hoped, by the teachers, that the children would become more aware of books and read more for pleasure. Not having to respond with reports/reviews was also regarded as important in encouraging the children towards reading. For some children at least this was successful;

> It makes me feel I should read more and more. (Sebastian)

Although there is no quantitative data to demonstrate the success of ERIC, the atmosphere in the school during ERIC time and the views of the staff and children suggest that it was worthwhile. Amongst the features suggesting success were; that the children were more aware of authors and that they now were reading longer books because there was time to do so;

> There is more time to read longer books. (Catherine)

Furthermore, as has already been noted some children wished that a longer time might have been available.

Of course, ERIC, or SQUIRT or any other variation of sustained silent reading, is only successful if the teacher provides an organization and commitment for the activity. Adequate materials, the link to a natural break, insistence on uninterrupted silent reading and the teacher providing a clear role model are all important. Furthermore, it is necessary to persevere. At first some children will find the sustained silent reading to be strange and they will need encouragement to overcome this strangeness. However, with such encouragement and support the children will gradually become accustomed to the event;

> I thought the silence was a bit funny at first but I have got used to it now. (Catherine)

The effect of sustained silent reading may well extend beyond the school. Many of the children commented upon reading more at home. Indeed one girl, Kavita, reported upon a period of silent reading known as KRIB. This was a period of time she had negotiated at home for Kavita Reading In Bed. Perhaps in due course RIB will become another well documented acronym to denote a sustained silent reading period, albeit this will be at home rather than at school.

A very important feature of sustained silent reading is then the apparent positive perceptions of the activity by the children. It is a time to enjoy reading. In addition the children are offered a time to read a longer section of a book than might normally be provided in school. They will see an adult engaged in reading, they have the opportunity to practice reading and they are able to choose the book they wish to read. Sustained silent reading provides an important contribution to the reading together continuum and the children demonstrate that importance in their own words;

> ERIC stands for Everyone Reading In Class, I enjoy ERIC very much and I look forward to it every day. ERIC was a brilliant idea and I wish someone could have thought of it earlier, then I could of had 10 minutes silent reading for 4 years if it had been thought of when I was in the first year. ERIC has encouraged me to read more at home because it shows how much fun reading can bring. (Stephen)

The role of the teacher

As has already been noted at a number of points in this chapter it is regarded as vitally important that the teacher reads together with the children during periods of sustained silent reading. In particular this was emphasized in the two examples that were explored above. These examples also reflect the views of theorists as, from the earliest writing about Uninterrupted Sustained Silent Reading (Hunt, 1970) and Sustained Silent Reading (McCracken, 1968), one of the key features which has invariably been put forward is that of the teacher as a role model. Indeed

McCracken went as far as to indicate that he had not seen one instance where the practice had failed providing that the teacher had read alongside the children.

Why should the teacher as a role model be of such importance? Perhaps it is because as teachers we can tell children to do certain things and then provide a demonstration to indicate that such an activity is of little importance because as teachers we do other things. Or we can, as teachers, say something is of importance and then show by our actions that we believe our own words by doing it as well. Children may well learn in part by observation and by imitation. As teachers we have the opportunity to demonstrate our interest in and enjoyment of reading by providing a role model of silent reading. Children will observe this reading and may well imitate such behaviour.

But is there any evidence that modelling actually works during sustained silent reading? McCracken and McCracken (1978) recognized the unscientific nature of their investigations but nevertheless claimed that unless all the adults in the classroom were reading then sustained silent reading would not work. More recently in one of the most detailed studies of the teacher providing a model of silent reading, Wheldall and Entwistle (1988) supplied some evidence; this was also briefly reported by Wheldall (1989). The study actually consisted of four separate but linked studies with groups of third and fourth year junior children. The first two studies provided convincing evidence of an increased amount of time spent reading by the children when the teacher also read and of a drop in reading when the teacher returned to other activities. In brief, there was a 20–30 per cent increase in the amount of time spent reading when the teacher also read. Typically, the amount of time spent reading moved from approximately 50 per cent to 70–80 per cent of the available time. Studies of individual children generally confirmed these findings although for two children with particular emotional/social problems the expected pattern was not followed. The fourth part of the study considered whether it was the teacher reading or the quietness associated with the teacher reading that encouraged silent reading. So over a period of time, the teacher either engaged in normal activities, read silently or wrote silently. The children spent most time reading while the teacher also read. However, during the time that the teacher wrote quietly, the children were also largely on task but not to the same extent as when the teacher modelled silent reading.

Mangan (1988) also explored pupil involvement in reading during periods of silent reading in a junior school. However, the organization of silent reading in that school was designed to coincide with registration periods. The teacher was, therefore, busily involved in administrative duties and subsequently in providing an organization for the school day. The individual children who were observed during these periods varied quite substantially in their involvement with the task of reading. Thus, although three children spent over 90 per cent of the time reading, two children during a 20 and 14 minute period respectively did not spend any time reading. Furthermore, there was some evidence to suggest that those children of low or average reading attainment were those who were likely to be distracted from reading while the teacher was involved in a variety of activities.

So for sustained silent reading to be effective the teacher has to read together with the children. Certainly in both the schools used as examples above, SQUIRT and ERIC, the teachers were unequivocal in their views. In order for sustained silent reading to be a success the teacher and any other adult in the room had to read. Some of the teachers noted that on the odd occasion when they had been diverted from providing a model of silent reading then the children were also less involved with their reading.

But not all teachers may be convinced of the need to be a reading model during sustained silent reading (Perez, 1986). And it is not hard to understand why this may be the case. The conscientious teacher is concerned about how just sitting and reading can be justified when there are so many tasks to be completed (Mork, 1972). Teacher comments from a recent interview exemplify the dilemma. A junior school teacher said;

> I think the teacher modelling during sustained silent reading does perhaps improve the children's concentration. If you are actually reading you do set them an example . . . I can't think of many teachers who actually do read. Most of them were shuffling papers of some sort . . . If you are doing something very quietly at your desk, this could be marking, it might not affect them too much . . . I think because they (the teachers) had so little free time . . . it was a time to . . . check up on all the little things you needed to do . . . I can see advantages for sitting and reading and ummm . . . I think I'll have to try it. (Scrivens, 1988)

These comments reflect the studies already cited; modelling may be best; working quietly may be an alternative which would be second best, but with so much to be done feelings of guilt may not always be avoided.

The evidence from a variety of sources, albeit limited, does suggest that for sustained silent reading to be a success the teacher will need to provide a model of silent reading. Of course, the teacher working as a role model will not guarantee success. There are other organizational aspects of sustained silent reading which are of some importance. And these organizational features will require the teacher's attention. Nevertheless as McCracken and McCracken (1978) concluded 'what a teacher does during and after silent reading defines silent reading for children' (p. 407). The teacher as a role model during sustained silent reading may be as important as that. And of course it reflects the continuation of the role of the teacher to guide, support and facilitate the children's reading during reading together. That support during silent reading is to show the children that not only do adults read but that they enjoy the activity. Indeed derived from that enjoyment the teacher will occasionally wish to share some of that which has been read with the children. And the children will wish to talk about their reading.

Although the teacher reading alongside the children is vital, McCracken and McCracken (1978) argued that what the teacher does after the reading time is also crucial. At the end of the allotted time the teacher might talk about what has been read, share a particular phrase or even read a short part of the story to the class. Each of these elements may provide a model of what is involved in reading. For instance at the end of one sustained silent reading session a teacher was observed (Scrivens, 1989) to say to her class of six-year-old children;

I've just been reading a very exciting bit in this book. Would you like to hear it?

The children responded positively and enthusiastically to the question. Therefore the teacher read an extract from 'James and the Giant Peach' in which James was experiencing terrible treatment from his aunts. The teacher then asked;

What do you think happened next?

The children were therefore being asked to predict the outcome. The children responded by making a number of suggestions, after which the teacher concluded by saying;

Would you like me to start reading this book to you in story time?

The children readily agreed to this and one child asked to borrow the book to look at.

Arising out of these teacher comments the children in the class would be encouraged to share their thoughts about the books that they had been reading. The adults and the learners would share their enjoyment of reading during this part of reading together.

Summary

In many classrooms children's silent reading may be in short bursts (Lunzer and Gardner, 1979) or limited in length (Southgate, *et al.*, 1981).

A period of time devoted to sustained silent reading is therefore suggested (Southgate *et al.*, 1981) This suggestion builds upon ideas mooted earlier by Hunt (1970) and McCracken (1971).

Although a number of acronyms are utilized to describe sustained silent reading the important feature remains that each learner will have an uninterrupted period during which material of the learner's choice can be read silently (Allington, 1975).

Three key aspects within the organization of sustained silent reading require careful consideration. These aspects are time, materials and guidance (Campbell, 1988b). A short but gradually lengthening amount of time linked to a natural break in the school day, a wide range of interesting and meaningful books and guidelines which include quietness with the teacher also reading were suggested.

The particular importance of the teacher reading together with the children was emphasized (McCracken and McCracken, 1978). And some evidence to support such a view was noted (Wheldall and Entwistle, 1988; Mangan, 1988).

After the sustained silent reading period the teacher may comment upon what has been read (McCracken and McCracken, 1978) and subsequently the children might want to talk about the books they have read (McCracken, 1971).

CHAPTER 6

Conclusion

Whatever ideas are put forward as suggestions to encourage children to read, or indeed for children to learn in other areas, the main ingredients for success may well be the competence of the teacher and the enthusiasm for the subject that is demonstrated by that teacher/adult. Reading together is no different in that it requires a sensitive and guiding adult and an enthusiasm for reading which is demonstrated in the stories read, the sharing of a book as the child gains independence as a reader and the involvement with sustained silent reading. This involvement during sustained silent reading includes the comments made following the read where the teacher will demonstrate the enthusiasm for reading and the enjoyment of it.

In attempting to get these ideas, of sensitive, competent teaching and enthusiasm for reading, into this book the cold print of text appears to rob the interactions which have been provided of some of the warmth and enthusiasm which has been witnessed by the author in numerous classrooms. However, many teachers may be able to reconstruct the events from the text and picture, more clearly, the collaborative literacy activities which have been debated.

Of course one of the problems related to providing suggestions, within the debate, about story reading, shared reading, hearing children read and sustained silent reading is that these suggestions begin to be seen as a checklist of points to be covered. As Campbell (1988a) noted such ideas should not be seen as prescriptive. Each teacher will need to consider the ideas expressed in this book in relation to the children in the class and to use professional judgements in determining how best to proceed. As we noted earlier Graves (1984) argued that orthodoxy can be the enemy. A simple application of guidelines can be detrimental to the dynamics of the interactions which have been debated. What has to be avoided is that the literacy activity becomes a ritualized event in the way that Goodacre (nd) suggested hearing children read had become for some teachers. The teacher and the learner need to be involved in a genuine shared literacy event in which at various points the learner will initiate comments and ideas to which the teacher will respond. Shared meanings and understandings will be developed during the teaching and learning process. Therefore a flexibility and responsiveness is required. This cannot be achieved if there is a strict adherence to perceived guidelines.

None of the reading together events can occur unless the teacher has first been able to organize the classroom for these literacy activities, and activities in other curriculum areas, to take place in a working atmosphere. The need for an adequate organization has been stressed in this book and quite simply this organization is required in order to create the time for the literacy activity to occur, and time may be an important factor that encourages reading development (Harris, 1979). Furthermore without the organization there may be too many interruptions directed at the teacher which would diminish the effectiveness of the reading together events. Southgate *et al.*, (1981), in particular, noted how the lack of an adequate prior organization led to disturbances of hearing children read interactions in the junior school.

In the school context, given that the organization has been considered adequately and executed, then the opportunity occurs for the various forms of reading together to occur in a worthwhile manner. The children will be encouraged to develop as readers by reading (Smith, 1978). And providing that the interactions are ones of genuine sharing then the teaching and learning can be successful. As Meek (1982) argued, the conditions for success are to be found in the teacher, the learner, a book and a shared enjoyment. And as has been argued within this text this shared enjoyment can occur during times of reading to and with children as part of reading together.

Nevertheless this success is dependent upon the teacher, the learner and a book. Each of these elements are important. The role of the teacher may not be to teach directly but it will have been noted throughout this book just how important the teaching role remains, or how more important and complex the role becomes. The teacher/adult will sustain, encourage and facilitate the child's reading development (Wells, 1985). A responsiveness to what the child is trying to achieve is crucial within these interactions. The teacher shares in the teaching and learning process and with careful guidance is teaching about reading. The support that the teacher gives in the form of subtle mediations are designed to encourage the child's development as a reader. And of course the learner is perceived as a self-activated learner who predicts possibilities and constructs meaning from books and does so with the guidance and support of the teacher. The child discovers about reading and to read using the knowledge of language and of the world that he/she brings to the task and increasingly uses the language cue systems within the text, partly because the teacher guides the child towards these systems and partly because the books being read help the child in his/her reading. As both Smith (1978) and Meek (1982) argued it is the use of meaningful books which can be a key factor in encouraging literacy development. Children will be motivated to read if the books they come into contact with are interesting, enjoyable and have a story to tell.

The eventual success of reading together is supported by the perspectives on literacy development which emphasize whole language (Goodman, 1986), emergent literacy (Hall, 1987) and interaction (Wells, 1985). Reading is developed or emerges over time as the child is involved with meaningful books and real stories. The learner is confronted not with separate and small skills to be learnt but with a whole language that supports the learning and encourages predictions and meanings within interesting and enjoyable books. This learning takes place as a social activity in which the interactions between the supportive teacher/adult and the inquisitive learner facilitates literacy development.

Of course the reading together continuum does not set the limits on all the opportunities for reading. Children will be involved in reading the environmental print of their surroundings, they will be reading to support the thematic work that they are engaged in within the classroom, they will browse and read in the library corner and these and other literacy events will support their development as readers. Furthermore, the children will be writing; this writing both grows out of reading and adds support to the child's development as a reader. So a whole range of activities will be helping the child in his/her literacy development. None of these activities have been debated in this book but their value is not denied.

Nevertheless a central strand of the support for a child as a developing reader can be reading together. The literacy activities of story reading, shared reading, hearing children read and sustained silent reading all have an important part to play in guiding the learners towards becoming readers and encouraging them to remain as readers.

References

Allington, R. (1975), 'Sustained approaches to reading and writing', *Language Arts*, Vol. 52. 813–815.

Allington, R. (1980), 'Teacher interruption behaviours during primary grade oral reading', *Journal of Educational Psychology*, Vol. 72. No. 3. 371–377.

Bergland, R.L. and Johns, J.L. (1983), 'A primer on uninterrupted sustained silent reading', *The Reading Teacher*, Vol. 31. No. 4. 406–408.

Bettelheim, B. and Zelan, K. (1982). *On Learning To Read*. London, Thames and Hudson.

Betts, E.A. (1946), *Foundations of Reading Instruction*. New York, American Book Co.

Bowermaster, M. (1986), 'It's time to SQUIRT', *Momentum*, Vol. 17. No. 4. 54–55.

Butler, D. and Clay, M.M. (1979), *Reading Begins at Home*. Auckland, Heinemann Educational Books.

Campbell, R. (1981). 'An approach to analysing teacher verbal moves in hearing children read', *Journal of Research in Reading*, Vol. 4. No. 1. 43–56.

Campbell, R. (1988a). *Hearing Children Read*. London, Routledge.

Campbell, R. (1988b). 'Is it time for USSR, SSR, SQUIRT, DEAR or ERIC? *Education 3–13*, Vol. 16. No. 2. 22–25.

Chapman, L.J. (1987). *Reading: from 5–11 years*. Milton Keynes, Open University Press.

Clay, M.M. (1979). *Reading: The Patterning of Complex Behaviour*. London, Heinemann Educational Books.

Cochran-Smith, M. (1984), *The Making of a Reader*. Norwood, New Jersey, Ablex Publishing Corporation.

Davis, C. and Stubbs, R. (1988a) 'Spreading the word', *Child Education*, April 1988. 42–43.

Davis, C. and Stubbs, R. (1988b). *Shared Reading in Practice*. Milton Keynes, Open University Press.

Dombey, H. (1987). 'Reading for real from the start', *English in Education*, Vol. 21. No. 2. 12–19.

Dombey, H. (1988). 'Partners in the telling', in M. Meek. and C. Mills (Eds), *Language and Literacy in the Primary School.* Lewes, East Sussex, The Falmer Press.

Fenwick, G. (1988), *Uninterrupted Sustained Silent Reading.* Reading. Reading and Language Information Centre.

Flood, J. (1977), 'Parental styles in reading episodes with young children', *The Reading Teacher*, Vol. 30. 846–867.

Gambrell, L.B. (1978), 'Getting started with Sustained Silent Reading and keeping it going,' *The Reading Teacher*, Vol. 32. No. 3. 328–331.

Goodacre, E.J. (nd), *Hearing Children Read.* Reading. Centre for the Teaching of Reading.

Goodman, K. (1986), *What's Whole in Whole Language?* Ontario, Scholastic-TAB Publications.

Goodman, Y.M. (1970), 'Using children's reading miscues for new teaching strategies', *The Reading Teacher*, Vol. 23. No. 5. 455–459.

Graves, D. (1984), *A Researcher Learns to Write.* Exeter, New Hampshire, Heinemann Educational Books.

Hall, N. (1987), *The Emergence of Literacy.* Sevenoaks, Kent, Hodder and Stoughton.

Harris, A.J. (1979), 'The effective teacher of reading revisited', *The Reading Teacher*, Vol. 33. No. 2. 135–140.

Heath, S.B. (1982), 'What no bedtime story means: narrative skills at home and school', *Language in Society.* Vol. 11. 49–76.

Hewison, J. and Tizard, J. (1980). 'Parental involvement and reading attainment', *British Journal of Educational Psychology*, Vol. 50. 209–215.

Hoffman, J.V. and Baker, C. (1981). 'Characterizing teacher feedback to student miscues during oral reading instruction', *The Reading Teacher*, Vol. 34. No. 8. 908–13.

Hong, L.R. (1981). 'Modifying SSR for beginning readers', *The Reading Teacher*, Vol. 34. No. 8. 888–891.

Hood, J. (1978). 'Is miscue analysis practical for teachers?' *The Reading Teacher*, Vol. 32. No. 3. 260–266.

Hudson, J. (1988). 'Real books for real readers for real purposes', *Reading*, Vol. 22. No. 2. 78–83.

Hunt, L.C. (1970). 'The effect of self-selection, interest and motivation upon independent, instructional and frustrational levels', *The Reading Teacher*, Vol. 24. No. 2. 146–151, 158.

Kaisen, J. (1987). 'SSR/Booktime: Kindergarten and 1st grade sustained silent reading', *The Reading Teacher*, Vol. 40. No. 6. 532–536.

Lunzer, E. and Gardner, K. (1979), *The Effective Use of Reading.* London, Heinemann Educational Books.

Mangan, M.P. (1988), 'An exploration of reading teaching and learning in the junior schools'. Unpublished BEd project. Hatfield Polytechnic.

Martin, T. (1989). *The Strugglers.* Milton Keynes, Open University Press.

McCracken, R.A. (1968). 'Do we want real readers?' *Journal of Reading*, Vol. 12. No. 6. 446–448.

McCracken, R.A. (1971), 'Initiating Sustained Silent Reading', *Journal of Reading*, Vol. 14. 521–524, 582–583.

McCracken, R.A. and McCracken, M.H. (1978), 'Modelling is the key to sustained silent reading', *The Reading Teacher*, Vol. 31. 406–408.

Meek, M. (1982), *Learning to Read*. London, Bodley Head.

Meek, M. (1984), 'Forward', in J. Trelease (Ed.), *The Read Aloud Handbook*. Harmondsworth, Middlesex, Penguin.

Meek, M. (1988), *How Texts Teach What Readers Learn*. Stroud, Thimble Press.

Mork, T.A. (1972). 'Sustained silent reading in the classroom', *The Reading Teacher*, Vol. 25. 438–441.

Perez, S.A. (1986), 'Children see, children do: teachers as reading models', *The Reading Teacher*, Vol. 40. 8–11.

Scrivens, G. (1988), 'SSR-Teacher interviews'. Unpublished report, SSR project, Hatfield Polytechnic.

Scrivens, G. (1989), 'What happens at the end of an SSR session?' Unpublished report, SSR project, Hatfield Polytechnic.

Sinclair, J. McH. and Coulthard, R.M. (1975). *Towards an Analysis of Discourse*. Oxford, Oxford University Press.

Smith, F. (1971), *Understanding Reading*. New York, Holt, Rinehart and Winston.

Smith, F. (1978), *Reading*. Cambridge, Cambridge University Press.

Southgate, V., Arnold, H. and Johnson, S. (1981), *Extending Beginning Reading*. London, Heinemann Educational Books.

Strickland, D.S. and Morrow, L.M. (1989). 'Interactive experiences with storybook reading', *The Reading Teacher,*, Vol. 42. No. 5. 322–323.

Teale, W.H. (1984). 'Reading to young children: its significance for literacy development', in H. Goelman, A.A. Oberg and F. Smith (Eds), *Awakening to Literacy*. London, Heinemann Educational Books.

Teale, W.H. (1988), 'Reading their way to reading', *Reading Today*, Vol. 5. No. 6. 18.

Topping, K. (1986). 'W.H.I.C.H. Parental involvement in reading scheme? A guide for practitioners', *Reading*, Vol. 20. No. 3. 148–156.

Trelease, J. (1984), *The Read Aloud Handbook*. Harmondsworth, Middlesex, Penguin.

Veatch, J. (1978), *Reading in the Elementary School*. New York, Wiley.

Wade, B. (1982). 'Reading rickets and the uses of story', *English in Education*, Vol. 16. No. 3. 28–37.

Waterland, L. (1985), *Read With Me: An Apprenticeship Approach to Reading*. Stroud, Thimble Press.

Wells, G. (1985), 'Language and learning; an interactional perspective', in G. Wells and J. Nicholls (Eds), *Language and Learning: An Interactional Perspective*. Lewes, East Sussex, The Falmer Press.

Wells, G. (1986), *The Meaning Makers: Children Learning Language and Using Language to Learn*. London, Hodder and Stoughton.

Wheldall, K. (1989), 'Reading USSR revolution', *Teacher's Weekly*, 20.2.89., 16–17.

Wheldall, K. and Entwistle, J. (1988), 'Back in the USSR: the effect of teacher modelling of silent reading on pupil's reading behaviour in the primary school classroom', *Educational Psychology.*, Vol. 8. 51–66.

White, D.N. (1984), *Books before Five*. Portsmouth, New Hampshire, Heinemann Educational Books.

Whitehead, M. (1987). 'Reading – caught or taught?' *English in Education*, Vol. 21. No. 2. 20–25.

Index